Are You a Candidate to Read This Book?

Take our quiz to find out. Simply mark Y for Yes or N for No on the line before each entry.

About You

___Some days you ask yourself, *Why do I bother to do nice things for my husband? He doesn't even notice them.*

___You wonder, *What's in it for me?*

___You fear the word *divorce.*

___Sometimes you just don't get him.

___Sometimes you feel like a hired servant (and your pay isn't worth it).

___You wonder if he really loves you, if he really cares.

___You're the one who always takes the initiative for anything you do as a couple.

___You feel like you're the only one holding the family together.

___You're not sure you really need—or want—your husband anymore.

___You wonder where your knight in shining armor went.

About Your Husband

___He never (or rarely) listens to you, even when you have something important to say.

___He's a good guy but clueless about how you really feel about anything.

___He never helps out around the house.

___When he's angry, he freezes you out.

___You ask him a question and you don't get an answer. You wonder if he's hard of hearing—or just ignoring you.

___He's singly focused on his work and other projects, and you don't seem to come into his radar.

___He doesn't give you much respect.

___He takes you and everything you do for granted.

___He is abusive in words and/or actions.

___He's a romantic no-show. (Flowers once a year on Valentine's Day just isn't enough.)

___He treats you like a slave, at his beck and call.

___You have to remind him over and over again if there's something you want him to do.

About Your Relationship

___Sometimes you wonder, *Where's the man I dated? The man I married?*

___Marriage isn't anything like what you'd dreamed of, and you have to admit you're disappointed.

___Late at night you wonder if your marriage is going to make it.

___You have active and continual conflict.

___The romance is long gone.

___Your communication could use some improvement. (You're a little tired of talking to yourself.)

___You wish your relationship was so much more than it is.

___You wish you had a great marriage like your best friend's.

___You're the only one trying to make the marriage work.

If any of these topics resonated with you and you marked even one Y, you need to not only *read* this book but *carry it around with you.*

This book will scratch where you itch.

I promise.

Have a new husband by Friday? Is it possible?

To tell you the truth, it's a scam. You can have a new husband by *Wednesday* if you do it right. Keep reading, and I'll show you how.

This is the miracle turnaround you're longing for.
I guarantee it.

Have a
New
Husband
by Friday

Have a New Husband by Friday

How to Change His **A**ttitude, **B**ehavior & **C**ommunication in **5 Days**

Dr. Kevin Leman

Revell

a division of Baker Publishing Group
Grand Rapids, Michigan

© 2009 by Kevin Leman

Published by Revell
a division of Baker Publishing Group
P.O. Box 6287, Grand Rapids, MI 49516-6287
www.revellbooks.com

Printed in the United States of America

Library of Congress Cataloging-in-Publication Data
Leman, Kevin.
    Have a new husband by Friday : how to change his attitude, behavior &
communication in 5 days / Kevin Leman.
        p.   cm.
    Includes bibliographical references.
    ISBN 978-0-8007-1912-8 (cloth)
    1. Marriage—Religious aspects—Christianity. I. Title.
BV835.L46 2009
646.7′8—dc22   2009008746

ISBN 978-0-8007-3307-0 (ITPE)

To protect the privacy of those who have shared their stories with the author, some
details and names have been changed.

To Mrs. Uppington, the best wife and friend I could ever have. I thank God for the day I met you (in the men's restroom), and that you said yes more than 45 years ago, in the field behind my parents' home. (I always was a romantic.) I know that as a little girl you prayed to someday have a man of character. But God has a sense of humor; he decided a character would do.

What a class act you are, Mrs. Uppington—a terrific mom and a delightful woman to share life with. It's been a great ride, hasn't it? What could be better than five great kids who love us and love each other? You've enriched not only my life with your beauty, strength, kindness, and thoughtfulness, but countless others.

With love, Leemie

Contents

Acknowledgments

Who said a man doesn't need a woman? In my case, I need lots of them, including these three wonderful women:

Jessica Miles, my Revell project editor, for her keen eye and helpful contributions that make this puppy sing.

Lonnie Hull DuPont, who somehow gives her work the personal touch and still keeps up with the flurry of projects passing her desk.

Ramona Cramer Tucker, who shares my passion for helping families build solid relational foundations—and encouraging them to smile and laugh along the way.

Introduction

Satisfaction Guaranteed

How would you like your new husband delivered? UPS, FedEx? (US mail is available, but at a slightly higher rate.) Or would you like him delivered via personal courier?

Do you remember those first euphoric moments you shared with your spouse after you'd become one? The dreams, the hopes, the desires that came along with that excitement? The nights you talked and cuddled in each other's arms BC (before children)?

But perhaps it seems like you're dredging up ancient history by this point. You've been married 5 years, 8 years, 17 years, or 27 years, and you've moved past euphoria and into reality (just long enough for the wedding flowers to wilt). You don't always like this guy you married. Some days he annoys you; some days he downright exasperates you. The last time you heard "I love you" was on Valentine's Day two years ago. You're tired of your "discussions," and you often seem to be at cross purposes. You wish he'd listen better, be a better daddy, and get off the couch every once in a while during football season.

You find yourself struggling to keep the marriage fresh and exciting. You've fallen into a rut. You wonder, *How did we get this way anyway?* Life with the knight of your dreams has turned into boredom with no hope of reprieve. You'd like to find a little excitement again.

Or perhaps you deal day in and day out with verbally or physically abusive or controlling men. You're beaten down, tired, and not sure if you want a new husband . . . at least not the one you have. You're ready to trade your old model in for good, but you've decided to give it one last-ditch effort to see if you want to save your marriage. (Hang on. I have a special section just for you.)

So many couples settle for so little in marriage when they could have so much. Don't fall for it. The truth is, after 10, 25, or 35 years, your marriage can be as rich and full and wonderful and exciting and sensual as you can possibly imagine! I ought to know. I've been married for over 40 years—in a row to the same woman—and we're still going as strong as the Energizer Bunny.

Some things in this book you'll like, others you won't. You can feel free to argue with me at any time. All I ask is that you hear me out. You picked up this book for a reason. The title attracted you. Who wouldn't want a new husband by Friday? Every woman is, at heart, a "Martha" Luther—a reformer. And she has plans for her man.

Is it possible? you wonder. *I've been working on him for years, and I've never been able to change him. Now this psychologist guy says I can get a new husband by Friday? This I gotta see! But if it works . . .*

Yes, the principles in this book do work. They've been tried out in thousands of relationships with very successful results. Best of all, they're simple. You don't need to schedule three luncheons with your girlfriends to discuss them and figure them out. Your man is a very simple creature. If you do a few things right and consistently to get his attention, you'll be surprised by how simple this really is. Hopefully *then* you'll call your girlfriends and say, "Hey, you're going to have to read this book. It works incredibly well!"

Follow these principles, and you'll have your new husband by Friday. He'll do anything for you. Got that? *Anything.* Covers the waterfront, doesn't it? That means you'll have a husband who wants to please you emotionally, intellectually, physically, and spiritually. He'll be your equal partner, helping out with any task that needs doing.

Have a New Husband by Friday is a simple game plan you can follow. It's not easy, but it's simple. The changes you'll see in your husband's attitude, behavior, and communication will astound you. I guarantee it.

It all starts with getting to know this two-legged creature you walked down the aisle with.

Monday

Secrets Revealed

Yes, you're different species, but you can work together in harmony.

"Hey, honey, where's the Weber's mustard?" I asked, standing in the kitchen with the door of the refrigerator wide open.

"It's right in the fridge," my wife said from two rooms away.

I attempted to cram more of my torso inside the door to look, then stood up again. "No, it's not."

"Yes, it is," Sande insisted, "on the right side."

I took another forlorn look, shrugged, and called again, "No, it's not."

I couldn't see Sande, but I could just imagine her rolling her eyes in slow motion. After all, this scene had played out countless times in our marriage.

Sande swept into the kitchen, walked to the fridge, opened the door that I had closed in despair, and grabbed the item I was searching for. "Could *this* be what you were looking for?" Mrs. Uppington said with an expression that conveyed how really stupid I was. Then she bounced back to her work, shaking her head.

Why is it that women always win at lost and found anyway?

Recently, my college daughter Hannah's roommate got engaged. I found out about it when I was talking with Hannah on the phone. I asked her, in typical male/father fashion, "Well, honey, what's new?"

"Oh, Becca, my roommate, just got engaged."

"That's nice," I said.

That was it. End of subject. Move on to the next one.

The next day Sande and I were in the car, and Hannah phoned her mother. Evidently she told her mother the same news, because Sande said excitedly, "Oh, what good news. That is so wonderful. Becca must be so happy, so excited!"

And so the long conversation launched. You know what questions I heard?

"Where did he give her the ring?"

"When are they going to get married?"

"Was she surprised?"

"Where's the wedding going to be?"

"Do her parents like him?"

"Are you going to give her an engagement party?"

"What does the ring look like?"

"Do you like it?"

"How do you feel about the engagement?"

Etc., etc., etc., with pauses in between for Hannah's excited chattering on the other end.

I just had to smile. There's definitely a difference between how men and women communicate. Hannah and I are close. We call each other often. But she shares with her mother differently.

Then there was the little encounter I watched yesterday. I was sitting at a restaurant in Elmira, New York, and right next to me was a table of two couples in their midthirties. The women were talking like two woodpeckers with ADHD. They shared continually, expressively, eyeball-to-eyeball, eight to ten inches apart, for the entire 45 minutes I was in the restaurant. Their husbands? They were doing the typical male behavior.

"Nice day, huh?"

"Yeah."

"Good soup."

A nod.

I couldn't help myself. I poked the guy next to me and said, "See those women? They're doing what they do best. They're *shaaarrring.*"

He grinned.

We both watched as the women got up from the table, and then, arm in arm as they walked out, they

> *Do my buddy Moonhead and I spend our times together intensely "sharing" from our hearts? Nope. We go fishing, we go to ball games. Exchanging guttural grunts and yelling "Get 'em!" is enough for us. But our wives? They're in "sharing and caring" mode, not to mention an occasional hug.*

talked about when they were going to get together again. "Well, Tuesday would work for breakfast, but Wednesday for lunch. But on Thursday they have a marvelous soup, so maybe Thursday?" They were still talking up a storm while their husbands, whose word count had been demolished in their brief exchange, trailed behind.

I could relate. As a guy, I call myself fortunate to have one really good friend who's been my buddy since we were three. But do Moonhead and I spend our times together intensely "sharing" from our hearts? Nope. We go fishing, we go to ball games. Exchanging guttural grunts and yelling "Get 'em!" is enough for us. But our wives? They're in "sharing and caring" mode, not to mention an occasional hug.

Then there's the fact that when I make dinner at home, there are ten-minute respites in between each course. "Corn!" I call out, and everyone comes to the table and eats corn. Ten minutes later, "Potatoes!" A good twenty minutes after that, "Okay, the meat's ready!"

Contrast that to my lovely bride, who whips off an incredible spread beautifully displayed. And even more shocking, all the food is done at the same time! (Hey, I even have to turn the radio down in the car when I'm looking for something. Multitasking just isn't my forte.)

> **Rules to Live By**
>
> 1. He's your husband, not your girlfriend.
> 2. He doesn't and never will think like you do.
> 3. He's equal but not the same.

There's no doubt about it. Men and women are different. If you don't believe that to be true, then you might as well put this book down now. You won't understand what I'm saying.

There's a mistaken notion in society today that *equality* means "sameness." Yes, men and women are equal, but one thing I'm positively sure of: they are *not* the same.

Equal but Not the Same

Men and women are clearly not the same. Our brains are different, our body chemicals are different, our emotions are different, and we see life from completely different angles. For example, the journal *Cerebral Cortex* reported that the part of the brain controlling visual-spatial abilities and concepts of mental space—skills necessary for tasks such as mathematics and architecture—is about 6 percent larger in men than in women.[1] Men's brains are larger, but women's brains contain more brain cells.[2]

According to studies, male and female brains work differently. When men and women perform identical tasks, different areas of their brains light up in response.[3] Females may use both hemispheres, while male brain activity is restricted to one side.[4] Researcher L. Cahill and colleagues discovered that left-brain memory activity is stronger in women, and right-brain activity is stronger in men.[5]

Left-Brain Functions	Right-Brain Functions
are logic oriented	are feeling oriented
are detail oriented	are big-picture oriented
focus on facts	focus on imagination
focus on words and language	focus on symbols and images
focus on present and past	focus on present and future
are math and science oriented	are philosophy and religion oriented
have good order/pattern perception	have good spatial perception
know object names	know object functions
are reality based	are fantasy based
can form strategies	can present possibilities
are practical	are impetuous
are safe[6]	are risk taking[7]

Have you wondered how your husband can work so long and so hard? Studies show that women have more severe and longer-lasting pain than men.[8] (But you already knew that, didn't you?) On average, you experience headaches, facial and oral pain, back pain, and other ailments more frequently and more severely than your husband does. Perhaps that explains why when you get the flu, you take DayQuil and keep going (you're used to putting up with a little pain), but when your husband gets the flu, he turns into a little boy who needs chicken soup and keeps yelling for orange juice, stat! Men can't handle pain the way women can.

Although a few researchers still try to pretend that men's and women's bodies are essentially the same outside the bikini lines, more doctors and scientists are coming to agree with Dr. Marianne Legato of Columbia University, who says, "We're talking about substantive, important differences between men and women in every system of the body, from the central nervous system to the gut, to the skin, to the way in which we metabolize drugs."[9]

These differences affect every area of marital life. For instance, about 31 percent of men experience sexual difficulty, compared to 43 percent (close to half) of women.[10] One study found that 1 out of every 3 women said she wasn't interested in sex, but only 1 out of every 6 men said the same thing. And 1 out of every 10 men reported that sex provides little pleasure for him, but 1 out of every 5 women admitted that sex isn't any fun![11] That's understandable, considering it's extremely rare for men to be incapable of achieving orgasm, yet lots of women consistently struggle in this regard.

The nature of sexual desire is equally distinct. You're probably not surprised that researchers have found that a man's sexual desire is "more easily triggered by external cues" (I can hear many of you sighing already) and is "more constant across the life cycle."[12] That's a fancy way of saying your husband will, on average, be easily aroused until the day he stops breathing! The same study indicated that a woman's sexual desire is much more reflective and reactive to her partner, rather than being spontaneous or initiated by her. In other words, her desire grows in interaction with her partner, while her husband's desire grows merely by seeing his wife naked—or with clothes on.

> Marrying a man is like buying something you've been admiring for a long time in a shop window. You may love it when you get it home, but it doesn't always go with everything else in the house.
>
> Jean Kerr[13]

No wonder that husband of yours is a foreign creature, an oddball, an utter (and sometimes exasperating) mystery. Knowing the way men are wired will go a long way toward helping you have a far more satisfying relationship. One thing's for sure: society isn't helping you out in this regard.

The Unisex Rip-off

Occasionally in this book, I'll step onto some "where angels fear to tread" territory. This is one such time. I ask that you hear me out before you jump to any conclusions or throw this book out the window. If your goal truly is to have a new husband by Friday, read on.

I'll be blunt. The whole feminist movement didn't do women any favors by pushing the unisex, "we're all the same, we're no different" philosophy onto the world. But frankly, we men are to blame. If we really were the kind of leaders the Almighty intended us to be, there never would have been a need for such a crusade. Both men and women would have existed in happy harmony.

Let me ask you: if you could have the perfect marriage, what would it look like? I'll paint a scenario, and you tell me what you think.

In a perfect marriage, the husband and wife have an intimate connection. They make joint decisions about life, talk about things before decisions are made, communicate love and respect to each other on a daily basis, and are able to talk about anything without fear of judgment, put-downs, or criticism. They have an intimate emotional connection. They could be away from each other for weeks due to work and come back and pick up a conversation right where they left off. They have a healthy and satisfying sex life. Their time together is as comfortable as their feet in a favorite pair of slippers on a cold winter night. They curl up in each other's arms, knowing they are loved, cared for, respected, appreciated, and listened to. Words don't even need to be exchanged all the time, because both husband and wife understand each other.

Marriage, at its core, is all about respect for the other person—and respect goes both ways. But today's culture disses men at every turn. Men don't get respect from anyone, let alone their wives. Sitcoms portray them as dolts who are so inept that they can't figure anything out, as buffoons who think through their fly. Actresses announce, "I'm going to have a child," but there's no mention of a father, a husband. The pervasive mentality in today's society is: "Who needs a man? They're good for nothing!" So that means men are left hanging out there, feeling they're not respected, not needed, and certainly not important.

> *Marriage, at its core, is all about respect for the other person—and respect goes both ways.*

Does such a mentality drive couples together or apart? Just look at the rising divorce statistics, and you'll have a clue. Today one out of two marriages ends in divorce, and the average marriage lasts only seven years. Lest you think your marriage couldn't be at risk because "we are deeply, *deeply* in love—we'd never get a divorce," that's exactly what other couples said—only seven years before they called their separate lawyers and started divorce proceedings.

So what's so different about you? How are you going to be different in order to keep your marriage together? To keep your husband in your bed rather than someone else's? To have a fulfilling, exciting, satisfying marriage that will stay that way until death do you part?

I can't count the number of times women have said to me, "But, Dr. Leman, I don't want to lose myself in marriage. I mean, I'm still who I am. I'm just married. I don't want to lose my identity." This is what I call the "married single's lifestyle." You're married, but you would never know it, except for the piece of paper that says you and your husband can now have sex legally. But you don't have an intimate connection, emotional vulnerability, or relational transparency because you're too concerned about "not losing yourself."

Interestingly, these women come into my counseling office because their marriages are in trouble. They lay out their problems, then say, "I want my husband to appreciate me for the woman I am—for my intellect, my creativity, etc., not just for my body or what I can do for him." As we talk further, I make some suggestions about ways they might want to interact differently with their husbands at home. Invariably, these women will respond, "You've got to be kidding. Please my husband? Now why would I want to do that?"

"Well then," my response is, "why would he want to please you?"

You see how it works, don't you? In a democratic society, if you have a right to put me down, then I have a right to put you down. If you don't feel like pleasing me, then I don't have to please you.

That's a recipe for marital disaster. If you're a person of faith, don't think you're immune. Ironically, the divorce percentage is even higher for people of faith, according to the Barna organization.[14]

So many couples today are living his-and-her marriages. Like his-and-her towels that look nice hanging up in the bathroom, that might work for a while. But give it a few years, and those towels start to look a little shabby. They start unraveling. So too do his-and-her marriages. The partners are so used to doing everything on their own that they start wondering, *Hey, why bother? I can do this without him (or her). I don't really need this marriage anymore.*

According to an article in *USA Today*, 42 percent of couples under 30 don't consult each other on major purchases (and that includes cars). If the husband wants it, he gets it. If the wife wants it, she gets it. (Interestingly, a third of those 65 or older say they share decision making in most major areas.)[15] No wonder so many married couples today are in the thick of financial troubles.

Yet in the midst of all this struggle for power in a unisex society, guess who rules the roost? No doubt, it's you women! And surprisingly, men aren't putting up a fight about it. Women have the upper hand at home, says another *USA Today* article:

> Of 1,260 individuals surveyed in four areas of decision-making in the typical American home, women had the final say in 43% of couples—almost twice that of men. . . .
>
> Megan Murphy, director of the marriage and family therapy program at Iowa State University-Ames, . . . [says,] "There's a myth out there that men are the heads of households and make the decisions, and that's it, but real life isn't like that, from what I see."[16]

Do you really want to be "the same" as your husband? Or do you want a guy who will see you as his equal partner in life—not the same as him but treasured because of how your differences work so well and excitingly together? He'll be the kind of husband who seeks you out for your brains and asks you what you think because he doesn't fear your judgment. He'll be the kind of husband who does anything for you. He'll take the garbage out (without being asked). He'll watch the kids so you can have a night off with your girlfriends. He'll be the companion you've always dreamed of—someone who listens to you, appreciates your intellect and ideas, and adores you. And that man who loves you will stick around for a lifetime. He'll be your knight in shining armor. He'll be your soul mate.

Guess who rules the roost? No doubt, it's you women! And surprisingly, men aren't putting up a fight about it.

Now, isn't *that* really what you want, when it comes right down to it?

So why not, for the remainder of this book, throw out any preconceived notions you have about who should do what in your home and who isn't doing what, and get to know this creature you've married? I promise you, it will be worth your while.

A Line in the Sand

Over the past several decades, society has been cleverly defining men's roles. The new "sensitive" man is supposed to be able to read a woman's mind (somehow picking up on a woman's intuition) and prefer to spend an evening cuddling and talking.

An evening of cuddling and talking is about as unnatural for a man as it is for a fish to climb a tree. When men get together, we talk about our jobs, the bills, the weather, the stock market, and the local sports team—anything that's one step removed from us. When a buddy tells us his wife just had a baby, we congratulate him, but usually we don't ask, "So how much did the baby weigh? . . . Nine pounds? Are you kidding me? That's a huge baby! Now, how long was the baby? . . . Twenty-two inches? The size of a nice walleye! Okay, tell me about the labor—how many hours?" That's just

> **How to Think Differently**
>
> 1. Assess the current situation.
> 2. What would you normally say? Is this helpful or harmful to your goal of having a new husband by Friday?
> 3. Before you say a word, make the commitment to respond differently.
> 4. Pair your verbal response with the body language to back it up.

not the way men think or talk. In fact, we'd probably forget to ask if it was a boy or a girl unless the proud daddy volunteers the information.

Men are physical beings. We're *attracted* to the physical. Here's what I mean. Think of the man you most admire and trust who's not a relative. Now put yourself in a situation where you meet this man socially. I can guarantee you something—in less than one-fifth of a second, this man has checked you out from your toes to your head and *all* major spots in between. Don't believe me? Ask your husband.

If we're honorable men, we won't mentally undress you. We won't imagine doing things with you that should be done only with our wives. But we *will* notice you. That's the way males are wired. We don't mean to offend you. We can learn not to leer or to make crude remarks. But most of us do look.

So, on behalf of all men everywhere, I'm drawing a line in the sand. I'm not going to any more Tupperware parties. I won't eat quiche. I won't apologize for thinking that sex and football are two of the Almighty's and man's greatest inventions (respectively). I might even stop this afternoon at a red light and spit out the window.

> *Don't fault your man for being a man. Testosterone has its advantages. How else do you think we get those mayonnaise jars open?*

I'm sick of getting in touch with my "feminine self." I like the masculine part just fine, thank you very much. There are some parts of my masculine body that I'm completely enamored with and proud of.

So that's the truth. What am I hoping to accomplish by telling you all this? I'll state it simply: don't fault your man for being a man. Testosterone has its advantages. How else do you think we get those mayonnaise jars open? But with the advantages of being a male also come the "disadvantages" that can drive women crazy. For instance, males think about sex far more than you realize—or maybe care to know. (If you do, it's 33 times more than you do.) We can never catch up with you in the sheer volume of words you produce; we're simply not capable of all that speech.

Boys have wildly different attention spans than girls. They prefer to look at objects for shorter (but more active) periods of time.

They're more intense and far more quickly bored. Their brains are wired to need to move more rapidly from object to object in space. That also means they take in less sensory information than girls do. (Hmm, perhaps that explains why your husband didn't notice your new haircut . . . until six months later.) They have three times more reading difficulties than girls and often develop their verbal skills almost a year later than girls.[17]

Men are different, and we *like* being different. I like not having to gather a group of reinforcements to back me up so I can visit the men's room in a restaurant. I'm perfectly happy going there by myself. And I'm sure *you're* perfectly happy being able to watch a television show without continually surfing all the other channels just to see what's on.

The Biggest Secret of All

But here's the biggest secret of all that you need to know about your husband. I've even asked the designers of the book to put it in bigger type so you don't miss it, since this fact is so very important.

He *wants* to be a good husband.

He *wants* to please you.

But he doesn't know how to do that.

He needs your help.

Surprised? I bet you are. Every bit of what I said is true. Even if you've been married ten years, that man of yours is still learning.

You see, he's spent X number of years being a man, but before that he was a little boy. When he first found out he liked girls, he figured out the best way to get that special girl's attention was to shove her or punch her shoulder. At least, that's how ten-year-old boys act, because that's the only way they know how to relate.

Boys are physical from the get-go. If you don't have sons and don't already know this to be true, just go sit at a playground sometime and watch children play. Make your own observations. Do you see girls tackling each other, jumping on each other's backsides, or wrestling balls away from each other as they roll on the ground? Nope. There also isn't a man on this earth who hasn't had a peeing contest with his buddies as he was growing up. Just ask your husband.

Boys and girls play and act differently. They are very distinct creatures as they grow up, and they continue to be those same distinct creatures in marriage. In the next chapter we'll talk more about that male creature, your husband, and how he got to be the way he is. But for now, suffice it to say that men are very elementary. They respond to the simple things of life. They respond to the power of touch. They respond to words that, for lack of a better term, build up their ego and make them feel important. This is especially important to men in today's milieu, which is busily tearing them down. These days, when a woman approaches a man in a positive way, you bet he takes notice!

Most men function as an island, not connected to anything. Each day they go to work or work from home, fulfilling their role to help provide for their family. They live in their own private world, not emotionally connected with anyone. But they're constantly thinking about things—such as the fact that the estimated tax due date is approaching. I think about those types of things all the time. They weigh on me. But Sande

> **What to Do on Monday**
>
> 1. Throw your expectations of your man out the window.
> 2. Evaluate: How is he like you? Different from you?
> 3. Think back. What attracted you to your husband in the first place? Make a list of those qualities.

doesn't think about those things. I tell her about them, but that doesn't have the same weight.

So when you believe your husband might not be thinking about anything, he's actually thinking very heavily about your future outside your home. He's not thinking about how to decorate the bedroom, where to go to get your daughter new shoes, what kind of salad dressing to put on the grocery list. He might be thinking about a statement his boss made at work about potential 5 percent cuts in salaries in order to keep the company afloat, and strategizing ahead of time about how to cut your own family's expenses as a result. He doesn't want to tell you yet, though, until he has it all figured out, because that's what males do. They're wired to problem solve.

Lest your hackles rose when I used examples of what you thought of as "domestic chores," here's a case in point. Recently I asked five women—two were stay-at-home moms, one worked part-time from home, and the other two worked outside the home full-time—what they think about during lunch. You know what? Each of those women listed multiple to-do items, and nearly all of those items had to do with domestic responsibilities: pick up the dry cleaning, shop for groceries, figure out where to go on vacation, find a carpet cleaner that really works, buy new shoes for Sally, etc. Although one of those "in the workplace" women was a corporate CEO and the other was a bank VP, they weren't thinking about their jobs during lunch. They were trying to juggle what they needed to get done at home and make a plan.

Now, I ask you, would any guy think about all those things during lunch? No, because males are wired to be singularly focused. That's why when you throw new information their way, you often get a "huh?" look. They're deep into the world of whatever they're thinking about and can't quite climb out of the pit to process anything new at the moment.

35

When I give seminars about the differences between men and women, I often ask, "How many of you men know what you're having for dinner tonight?" I get blank stares back. Not a single hand raises.

Next I ask the ladies. "How many of you know what you're having for dinner tonight?" Nearly every single female hand in that audience goes up. I add, "And you probably already have the main dish cooking in the Crock-Pot, don't you? Bet you've even planned to have color on the plate and to have every food group represented too."

Everyone in the audience laughs. I've made my point loud and clear. You are the efficient multitaskers of the century. No wonder you scare the pants off us men sometimes. You are so efficient that we wonder if we're needed in your world.

Women Talk

I never knew how much my husband needed me until I heard you talking about friendship. Then it hit me. Rob doesn't have any personal friends—none. He's not even close to his brother or his two sisters. He doesn't talk to anyone—except for me. Wow. As you pointed out, that's an awesome responsibility. Whoever thought about being a good friend to your husband? It made me realize that I have to let him know how much I need him in my life (I really do) and how much I respect him. I know I don't always do it right, but my trying has made a difference. He's not only coming home on time from work, but he just got a raise on the paycheck he brings home every two weeks. He's been a salesperson, kind of middle-of-the-road in his sales, but all of a sudden his sales volume has leaped. He seems so much more confident.

Tina, Colorado

What Your Husband *Really* Wants from You

Men are simple creatures compared to you complex females. There are only three things your husband desires from you, in this order:

1. He needs to be respected.
2. He needs to be needed.
3. He needs to be fulfilled.

He Needs to Be Respected

Respect is a huge issue for all human beings. But it is crucially important to men, especially in today's society. With men being portrayed as buffoons, it's no wonder so many slink into the background and become couch potatoes. (Though I certainly don't condone or excuse their behavior, I also understand why it happens.) Look at it this way: you're so good at everything you do that anything your guy does seems to pale in comparison. You can simultaneously change the baby, talk on the phone, kiss the baby's cheek, and make a doctor's appointment for your husband—all within the two minutes' time it takes your husband just to find the phone directory for the doctor's number.

At work, more and more of you are becoming doctors, lawyers, pilots, and CEOs. It's no wonder. You're marvelous whizzes at everything you do, and you can clean guys' clocks in accomplishing so many things that you're rising to the top easily.

Women Talk

I've gotten our family into some very serious financial difficulty because of my spending. My husband probably should have put his foot down years ago. In hearing you talk about how important it is to respect your husband, I was convicted. I've been selfish and not respectful to my husband, who works very hard to support us and our girls. I'm not exaggerating. He would go around and turn off lights that I left on just because I didn't want to bother turning them off. I finally apologized. I told him I was going to try to do better. I've never lived a disciplined life, but I'm finally trying to do so. I asked my husband to help me make a budget and bought some CDs from an author who specializes in finance.

My husband and I are now working together on our finances. It's hard, I'm not good at it, but I'm learning. And because I'm trying to do my best now, my husband has done a 180 toward me—I can see it in his eyes.

Maggie, Tennessee

Here's the rub. The man who feels dissed by his wife will sit back and think, *No way, no how, am I offering to help. She'll just tell me what I'm doing wrong and how I should do it better. I can never measure up to her, so why should I even try?* So there he sits, in front of the boob tube, as his wife rushes around, getting frantic because there's so much she needs to get done.

But the man who feels respected by his wife will sit back in absolute amazement and appreciation and watch her juggle. He'll express that by saying, "Honey, I can't believe all you got done today. You're simply amazing." Then he'll take it a step further. "What can I do to help?"

Let's call a spade a spade. There is no way, no how, that the accomplishments of us men in a single day can hold a candle to the huge fires you women put out on a daily basis. What's even more amazing is that 72 percent of you carry on all your family responsibilities and also work outside the home—and still somehow manage to make our world go round! Everything you do seems so effortless to us. You have a memory that doesn't quit. Somehow all those birthdays, anniversaries, and papers that need to be signed for school all get taken care of, and right on schedule. We can't begin to compete with that.

That's why respect is the #1 need for us men. Keep in mind that we *want* to please you (the little boy who wanted to please his mama has never quite grown up), but we know we can't come close to competing with you in what we do. Still, the little-boy heart in all of us longs for your respect—your belief that we indeed are capable, worthy human beings, and that we're important in your world.

Without respect, there is nothing to build your marriage on. There's no foundation. If you can't respect your husband, you might as well call it quits, because your marriage isn't going to make it.

Here's the even bigger issue behind respect. A man needs to feel your respect in order to love you the way you want to be loved. If he doesn't feel your respect, he won't climb out of his turtle shell to risk loving you because he might get hurt.

Ask Dr. Leman

Q: My husband never wants to go anywhere. He likes to stay home and putter around. A friend of ours is having a big barbecue in a month, and everyone we know is going. It would be a great time to catch up with our friends. But my husband said, "No, I don't want to go." He's so stubborn sometimes. How can I get my husband to see that doing things with friends, as a couple, is important to me?

A: When you and your husband were dating, what did you like to do? Did you do a lot of social activities with friends, or did you do quiet things with just the two of you, like having dinner, watching movies, taking walks through the park? Your husband may be an introspective guy who doesn't like the social scene. If you're a social butterfly who likes action and being surrounded by others, that can cause problems in your marriage.

Why not talk to your husband? Tell him it's important to you to do some things together with friends, and it means a lot to you to have him by your side at those events. Ask him if he'd be willing to go with you to the barbecue, but for a shorter time—perhaps one and a half hours instead of the four hours it usually takes. Tell him that when he gives you the high sign, you'll leave immediately. If he still says no, tell him, "Honey, I respect your decision. I understand it's not really your thing. But I'd still like to go. Would you mind if I went for a couple hours, and after I come home we could watch a movie of your choice?"

If your husband isn't wired to enjoy social interaction and he was like that when you married him, give him a break. Don't force him into situations where he's uncomfortable and withdraws from you or gets grouchy. Is his being with you at the barbecue really worth that?

Also, are the friends at the barbecue just your friends, or friends of both of you? There's a vast difference. If you're teaching college and always around highly educated folks, and he works in a diesel machine shop and is always around blue-collar workers, your guy could feel a bit intimidated if surrounded by all your colleagues and friends.

If your husband used to be a social creature but has withdrawn from activities with others, probe gently. "Honey, I noticed that you don't like to do activities with friends anymore. I could be wrong, but I'm wondering if something is bothering you and if there's anything you'd like to talk about."

Give those methods a try.

Then again, there are some men who don't deserve your respect because there is nothing to respect about them. They are crude, rough, and abusive. They treat women—you included—as a doormat to wipe their boots on. They don't respect you, and they make that clear in their daily treatment of you. If that's the situation you find yourself in, read on. You don't have to put up with such behavior. You shouldn't put up with such behavior. God almighty did not put you on this earth to be a doormat. You are a worthy, valuable human being. You'll find the next chapter very helpful in what you should do next to combat this type of behavior in your home, because it has to stop.

But the average husband wants to please you; he just doesn't know how. Of course you're better at a lot of things, but does that mean you shouldn't allow him to try? For example, I saw a father who, for the first time, diapered his 1-year-old son. As the child toddled off down the hallway, the diaper began its slow slide down to the carpet until the child, naked as a jaybird, began to run gleefully down the hallway, right into his mama's arms. You know what that wife did? She looked at her husband, wiggled her eyebrows, swept the child up with a laugh, and said, "Not so fast, big boy. Your daddy's ready to give your bottom another shot." And as that wife transferred that bare-bottomed child to her husband, she whispered in her husband's ear, "That was a great first try. I'd sure love to see *your* bare bottom later. Think we can plan on that?"

Now that's the smart wife. What did she do? She respected her husband's efforts to help (as inefficient as they were) and gave him the promise of reward for those efforts. Do you think that husband will be eager to help her with anything else that needs getting done? You bet. And as he does it, he'll be smiling ear to ear, thinking, *Wow. What a woman. And she chose me.*

Do you think that man will find himself being turned on by a co-worker who gives him a nice compliment? Nah. He'll just say a quick thanks and brush on by, because he can't wait to get home to *his* woman.

Right about now, some of you are saying, "Okay, Dr. Leman, stop right there. Everything you're saying so far has to do with what *I* have to do to get a new husband by Friday. So what about my husband? Doesn't he need to do his share of work in the marriage?"

Yes, he sure does. But here's the catch: your husband won't do his part until you do yours. That's because it's too risky for him, as a male, to try to do something when he doesn't know if it will be accepted.

Do you want the kind of husband who will listen patiently as you tell him about the idiots at work who are driving you up the wall? Do you want to be able to tell him anything and know that he'll understand? That he's there for you? When you talk to your husband, most of the time you don't really want him to solve your problem, do you? After all, you're a smart woman. You can figure it out.

> *Here's the catch: your husband won't do his part until you do yours.*

Most likely you know what you want to do already. But there's something wonderful about being able to share with your husband your thoughts and feelings, getting a warm hug of comfort, and hearing, "I'm sorry. That must be hard. I understand. Anything I can do to help you right now?"

Do you know how hard—and unmale-like—that is for a man? It's a male's first inclination to problem solve, to say to you when being presented with a problem, "Okay, here's what you should do . . ." and begin to tick off three immediate things you should act on. But respect is about understanding the other person, knowing how they tick (and what ticks them off), and what they're really asking for when they tell you about a situation.

But guess what? Your husband isn't as sensory oriented as you are, as studies show. That means he needs you to help interpret situations for him. He needs you to tell him, "Honey, I want to tell you about something that happened today with X. I don't need you to solve it for me, I just need you to listen."

You know what your husband will do? He'll perk up. He'll listen. You've just told him there's a problem and whom it's with (and since it isn't with him, he won't be on the defensive), and you've given him the assignment (to listen rather than problem solve), so he's at his male forte. He'll do as you ask.

Women Talk

If I knew it was this simple, I'd have tried it years ago. The other day I caught my husband vacuuming. Vacuuming! We've been married 22 years, and I've **never** seen the man vacuum. If I run to the store and leave dishes on the table, the table is clean and the dishes are washed by the time I get home. All because I started to tell my husband how much I need him. Your plan really works.

Phyllis, New York

He Needs to Be Needed

Think about how many friends you have—people you see on a regular basis, enjoy spending time with, go to lunch with.

Now think about how many close friends your husband has—and I'm not talking about the co-workers he says good morning to when he snags his cup of coffee in the break room. I'm talking people who know him really well.

Got it? Chances are high that it took you both hands to count all the friends you have. Then there's your husband. If he's a fortunate man, he has one close guy friend. For me, it's my buddy Moonhead. We go way back. But unlike our wives, we don't spend our time "sharing" our hearts. We don't spend hours talking—though we do have a record of 36 minutes in a row, on a very serious subject. But that's rare.

Most of the time, your husband has one friend. Guess who that is? You. See why it's so important that you respect him, as we talked about in the last section?

Your husband needs to be needed. Not by just anyone, but by you. You figure much higher in your guy's thoughts and life than you might think.

When you show your husband that you need him in your world, you trigger his God-given drive to provide, to help, and to solve problems. That's what a man likes to do best. He's a natural at it. That's why your husband sometimes drives you crazy telling you that you should do X, Y, Z in certain situations. That's his way of taking care of the problem and thus showing he cares for you.

> *Your husband needs to be needed. Not by just anyone, but by you. You figure much higher in your guy's thoughts and life than you might think.*

Shut off that problem-solving ability, and your man no longer feels needed. He feels criticized and put down, and he backs off quickly. You no longer have a helper; you have a reticent, sulking child to deal with. (I'm not proud of this truth about men, but a fact's a fact, and I'll admit to it in my own behavior. Just ask Sande.)

When it gets down to brass tacks, your husband doesn't have a lot of close personal friends with whom he socializes and talks. He has you. And oftentimes you're stressed. You have a career and multiple things to accomplish for the day. Add a kid or two or three in the mix, and how does your husband feel? Like a little puppy with sad eyes who's left behind in the corner, just hoping someone will look up and see him and take him for a walk.

It all goes back to the fact that your tough guy isn't as tough as he looks. Buried underneath all that bravado is a sensitive heart that fears being hurt.

Showing your husband he's needed is almost an art form. But it's so easy, and the results are worth the effort. When you see your husband in the evening, tell him, "Honey, I'm so glad you're home. Today's been a really stressful day, but all I could think about was getting to see you tonight again. I'm so glad I married you." Then slip him the commercial. "After you change clothes, would you mind helping Caysie with her homework while I finish up dinner? Then she'll be able to get to bed on time, and we can relax a little together."

Again, that's a smart woman. First she tells him she's glad to see him. (What guy doesn't want to hear that?) Next she tells him the day has been stressful and asks for his help with a specific thing. Then she promises him a reward at the end—time with her, the one he cares about the most and feels most comfortable with. What does she get in return? A happy husband who feels needed, who hurries home to her, and who helps out however he can.

Your words take so little time, but they mean so much. They're like rubbing a puppy's belly. They're the "ahh," the "attaboy." They're the catnip that makes the cat go crazy and be attentive to your every move. They're what will help you attain your purpose of having a new husband by Friday.

> *Sex is very important to a man. But it's not the only thing. There's ESPN too.*

Your guy needs you to be efficient and independent (as you already are)— just not *too* efficient and independent. He needs to know he has a solid place in your world, in your home, and in your arms.

He Needs to Be Fulfilled

I can already see some of you rolling your eyes at this one. *Oh, brother, here it comes*, you're thinking. *You're going to talk about sex now, aren't you, Dr. Leman? After all, that has to be just about the only thing a guy thinks he needs to be fulfilled.*

Well, you're wrong—and you're right. Sex is very important to a man. But it's not the only thing. There's ESPN too.

I'm kidding, but only partly. Think of it this way. When your guy chose you, he did so for a reason. He was thinking, *Hey, I found the woman of my dreams. I'm going to love her forever, and we're going to have great sex. Got the marriage job done.*

Then you got home from the honeymoon, and jobs crowded in, relatives crowded in, financial reality crowded in, and perhaps a child or two crowded in. Your guy got so busy providing for the family that he didn't pay as much attention to you along the way. (Even if you are working outside the home or making more than your husband does, your husband is the one who feels the pressure to be the provider for the family—that's just the way males are wired to think.) You've started to feel more like a servant than a treasured wife and lover. You're tired because of all your multiple responsibilities, and most nights you're too pooped to whoop.

But sexual fulfillment is extremely important to a man. Notice that I said "sexual fulfillment," not just "sex." There's a difference between simply having sex and being sexually satisfied. Many men and women run from person to person, having sex, just to find sexual satisfaction that lasts. But I will state it boldly: satisfying sex can be found only in the bounds of marriage, where both husband and wife have committed to love each other and stay together for a lifetime. Sex outside the bounds of marriage is not safe or emotionally satisfying (though it may be physically satisfying temporarily).

So here is this man who has chosen you—even with the few pounds you've gained since you met and married—to be his sexual partner. But just being a sexual partner isn't enough. He needs you to be a *willing* sexual partner. He needs to be needed. Sexual fulfillment affirms the very core of who a man is—it affirms his masculinity. It intensifies his drive to protect you, to care for you, to love you, to provide for you. If you are intimate with your husband, he will seek no other. Otherwise you put him at great risk for being vulnerable and falling into someone else's arms. Is that what he should do? No, but it is often what happens. That's how affairs start. A little appreciation or a simple compliment can turn into a torrid affair that can pull your marriage apart.

If you choose not to have sex with your husband, does that justify him having an affair? Absolutely not. That's not what I'm saying. A person doesn't fall into an affair; he or she chooses to have an affair. And if your husband has done so (many of you reading this book will know what I'm talking about), he has made a devastating choice—for him and for you. (We'll talk more about this later.)

What I am saying is that sex is important to your husband, even if it doesn't rank high on your priority list. (We'll talk more about that later.)

So make time for this very important aspect of your relationship. And don't wait for him to initiate sex. Take a risk. Pursue him.

Ask Dr. Leman

Q: My husband has a big business dinner every year, and I go out of my way to look nice. After all, these are people he works with on a daily basis, and many of the supervisors and regional directors are there too. So I always have my hair done, buy a nice dress, do my nails. You'd think he could say, "You look nice." But no. Nothing. I'm really frustrated.

A: You need to talk straight with your husband. "I just did a little math. That was the ninth awards dinner I've attended with you for your company. For nine years I've done my hair, gone out of my way to find a dress—on sale—and always tried to look nice for you because I know these people are important to you. But I need to know something. Is it important to you that I look nice, or can I just throw something on this year?"

He's going to look shocked, then he's going to say, "Well, no, I want you to look nice."

Then you can say, "Would it ever strike you that I'd like to hear you say I look nice? In order to get my hair done, I have to arrange for a sitter for the kids. I have to take them along to the mall to find a dress. Oh, that's a lot of fun. Maybe you don't realize how much time and effort goes into me trying to look nice. When you don't say anything to me, it makes me feel like I don't count, like you don't notice or appreciate me. So I'm asking you and myself at the same time, is it worth it? If it's not important to you, I'll just throw myself together and comb my hair."

That'll turn your man around. He needs a wake-up call. Men enjoy a lot of things and never comment on them. He needs to know what's important to you.

Above all, affirm his masculinity. Even men who are physically unable to have sex because of disabilities or ailments love to be stroked in various places. What your man needs to hear is, "I want you. I need you. You are my man." That is sweet music to his ears.

In all my years as a therapist, I've never had one man who has been respected, needed, and fulfilled by his wife come to my office to seek a divorce. If it happens, I've never seen it. Why? Because those three basics are the foundation for your husband to be the man he's intended to be. And you'll be much happier and more satisfied in every respect because you paid attention to those key basics.

They're oh so simple—but not easy. It takes a smart woman to realize that her husband doesn't need a lot, he just needs a little. If you meet his needs in these three areas—you respect

What Men Need Most	What Women Need Most
1. To be respected	1. Affection
2. To be needed	2. Honest, open communication
3. To be fulfilled	3. Commitment to family

him, need him, and fulfill him—you will gain that new husband you long to have.

What You Need More Than Anything

We've just talked about your husband's top three needs—to be respected, needed, and fulfilled by you. But what about a woman's? What do you long for more than anything?

You women have three top needs, in this order:

1. You need affection.
2. You need honest, open communication.
3. You need commitment to family.

Quite different from your husband's top needs, aren't they? See how different the two of you are emotionally, and why sometimes you rub each other the wrong way?

You want to snuggle and hear sweet somethings in your ear; he can't kiss your neck without you ending up flat on your back because he's wired to complete the act of sex. You crave hearing about his day and want to tell him all about yours; he's giving you guttural responses because he's problem solving what to do about the raccoon knocking over the garbage can every Monday. You want him to show up at your son's Little League games; he's late because he has to finish a project at work that will give him the edge over a colleague for a potential raise and new title.

See what I mean? So why not acknowledge your differences and take a little pressure off? And have a little fun along the way?

Bob Costas, a great sports announcer, has a spot on the radio that's sponsored by JCPenney. Whoever wrote the commercial really understands men: "JCPenney makes it easy for you to get in, find it, and get out." I was tickled when I heard that.

Then there's my wife, who leaves tomorrow for Phoenix to go shopping. Evidently Tucson stores are inferior, so she has to drive 115 miles to shop.

I'm a go-for-the-gusto kind of guy. I get on the road and enjoy the competition of driving. I know where I'm going and have my destination solidly fixed in my mind.

Then there's Sande. Once she was driving home with our daughter Hannah from Buffalo, New York. All of a sudden Hannah saw a sign and said, "Uh, Mom, we're in Pennsylvania." Sande had missed the turnoff. But you know what? That smart woman of mine just laughed. She wasn't defensive; she didn't take it badly that she'd driven past interstate 86 and ended up in good ol' Pennsylvania. I guess those big red, white, and blue interstate signs are difficult to see when you're "sharing."

It's one of the many things I love about Sande. She's incredibly fun, she's sweet, and she's talented in completely different ways than I am. Most of all, she shows me every day in multiple ways that she respects and needs me and does her best to fulfill me.

If you want a new husband by Friday, you have to understand just how tremendous an influence you have over your man, even if he doesn't act like it or admit it. For instance, Sande can say to me, "Oh, that's an interesting combination you have on, Leemie." And I know immediately what that means. It translates, "You didn't dress right. Please go change." My fear is that I'll be at my funeral, laid out in my casket, and she'll peer over the casket and say, "You're not wearing that."

You see, we're different. Sande gets up in the morning, takes time to groom herself, does her hair, etc., so she's always at her best. Me? I get up, put on a T-shirt, a baseball cap, and the shorts I wore the previous day. I brush my teeth and take my medicine, and I'm out the door. Notice that I didn't need to comb my hair. Why? It's simple: I'm wearing a hat. Why would I need to comb my hair?

My life, as a man, is simpler than Sande's. I don't deal with "that time of the month," and most days I don't have to think about dinner, unless I'm taking her to dinner someplace. And before you protest that I'm saying the woman always has to be the cook in the family, let me state for the record: everyone in the Leman family knows that Sande is a much better cook than I am, and she enjoys cooking.

Women Talk

*In my ten years of marriage I tried to please my husband. But it wasn't until I heard you on a TV program that I realized in trying to please my husband, I always expected something specific in return. When I stopped expecting my husband to pay me back, I found something really interesting: I started to **enjoy** pleasing and surprising my husband. I'm amazed at what's happened in our home. My husband has pleased **me** more in the last three months than in ten years of marriage! That's brought the fun back into our marriage.*

Cindy, Texas

I also have an assistant (a firstborn woman who's very good at what she does) who keeps this baby of the family on time for all his appointments, speaking engagements, and radio and television shows. Somehow Sande manages to juggle all the tasks of her days without an assistant, and I'm continually amazed.

So, with all the differences between male and female creatures, is it possible not only to coexist but also to complement each other? You bet. Sande and I are a living testimony of that every single day. And we're about as different from each other as you can get.

Some folks today, if given a shot at getting married all over again, would say, "I'd marry someone different." But not me. I'd choose Sande all over again. You see, we've learned that by putting the other first, we've formed a union that won't quit, that doesn't consider divorce an option, and that is joyful every day. Do we irritate each other sometimes? Sure. We're only human. But do we laugh a lot? Definitely.

So if you're asking, "Dr. Leman, you mean I have to put my husband first?" well, yes, that's part of what I'm saying. But I'm also saying that he has to put you first. That's what marriage is all about. It's not about two selfish parties wanting their own way; it's about a partnership of two people working together for their common good.

Most guys are as dumb as mud about what to do to make you happy. But they're sure willing to try. So why not give your guy a chance and see what can happen if you respect him, need him, and fulfill him?

Tuesday

Creatures from Another Planet . . . or Creatures of Habit?

To understand men, you have to track 'em to their den.

When my buddy Moonhead and I were seven or eight years old, we hatched a scheme. Well, another scheme, since we were always up to something. We decided that we wanted to catch a rabbit. So we took a box out into the field, tilted it at an angle, and propped it up with a stick. Underneath, just inside the box, we put some lettuce and a carrot. To our thinking, that dumb little bunny was going to come hopping by, see the carrot, go inside, knock over the little stick holding the box, and voilà! The box would fall down like magic, and we'd catch ourselves a rabbit.

Talk about dumb and dumber.

But women occasionally make the same mistake by assuming they can rag on their man to turn him into a better husband. Pestering their husband to change is like trying to catch a rabbit without first studying what the critter is, where it feels most comfortable, and what it likes in its habitat.

Think of your husband as a creature for a moment. A creature who is in a very different phylum than you (if you remember your Biology 101 from high school).

Yeah, he's a creature all right. A creature from another planet, you might be saying about now. If you are, congrats! You're on second base already. You're going to make great progress because you understand that male of yours is a different creature physically, emotionally, and psychologically.

Physically, it's easy to see the differences. That doesn't take a brain surgeon, just a swift look at a couple of body parts. He has testosterone; you don't. You have estrogen; he doesn't. He would probably wear the same clothes day after day, week after week, if you'd let him. He's had those favorite jeans for seven years now, the ones with the big wallet indentation in the back pocket. That doesn't seem to bother him—but it does bother you. Compare how many shoes you have on your side of the closet to how many shoes are on his side. He's very predictable. He'll order the same food at the same restaurant (he rarely gets sick of anything) without looking at the menu, but you like to look over the menu for a while and choose something new to try. He reads the newspaper the same way every morning; you read articles that catch your eye.

Psychologist Karen Sherman sums up the differences between men and women and how they play out in relationships:

> Women and men process information very differently. . . . Women's brains are wired to respond to more subtle non-verbal cues. They also use 20,000 forms of communication a day (verbal and non-verbal) as compared to a male's typical 7,000! Men's brains are slightly larger in size but women's brain's have more neural connections. Men use one hemisphere to process information while women use both.[1]

So what does this mean? If you, as a woman, are giving your guy hints about something you want him to do, and he's not getting it, it's because he's wired to be . . . guess what? A man! But make a direct request and he'll most likely hop right on it—*if* you need him, respect him, and fulfill him.

Part of the problem for both men and women in relationships is simply this: a man thinks he understands a woman, and a woman thinks she understands a man. But I want to let you in on a little secret: you don't understand your husband nearly as well as you think you do.

If you want to test me on this, write down a list of what you think is most important to your husband. Then ask him. You'll probably get a few right if you're a good observer, but chances are also good that you'll have a lot of surprises. How could there not be? You've never been a male, after all!

How can you best understand your man? Just as you learned about critters in science class by identifying them and then observing them, getting to know the creature that is your husband and observing him in his habitat can be extremely helpful in increasing your understanding of him as a male. Think of it as going back in time on your own personal safari, because who your husband is starts with who he was as a little boy and what his habitat was like.

The Little Boy He Once Was

Your husband's experience as a little boy has had a profound impact on who he is now as a man. The way his mother treated him, the way his male peers respected him (or didn't), and the way others looked on him—all combined to create the man you married.

It all intensified with your husband just before he hit puberty. One of the toughest acts on earth is being a boy between the ages of eight and fifteen. By the time he's eight years old, a boy is no longer considered cute and certainly not adorable. If your husband was anything like me, he probably looked a little funny, maybe even a little creepy.

Have you ever noticed how body parts grow at different speeds? Ears can overtake the head, for instance, or the head can overtake the body, creating a truly comical character. Not to mention the damage a well-placed zit can do to any adolescent's self-esteem.

While such a boy is too big to be adorable, he's too little to get any respect. He doesn't have biceps to speak of, so older boys will push him around. He is slowly, painfully changing from a boy to a man, so he's struggling with a Porsche-size engine in the body of a Hot Wheels car.

Then it happens. Your husband wakes up one day around seventh or eighth grade and finds his first pubic or chest hair, but it probably isn't soon enough (or thick enough) to keep him from humiliation in the school showers. There, the older, fully-haired, fully-developed Neanderthals snicker at the, ahem, less-than-gigantic proportions of Johnny's little jimmy.

When I was in junior high swim class, the boys swam in the nude. We'd come out of the locker room, naked as jaybirds, and sit on the edge of the pool until the teacher finished taking roll. One guy in that class, Alan, was hairy from head to toe, like an orangutan that hasn't had a haircut in a long time. He was huge in every significant place—and fully a *man*. Guess who had to sit right next to him during roll call? Little Kevin Leman, whose skinny white chest had a sum total of one hair—a little spaghetti noodle that I was tempted to darken with a felt-tip pen so everyone could see it. Let's just say that as I looked down below my waist, well . . . I looked every bit a boy. See why boys learn early that competition is the name of the game?

It's interesting that in a recently built high school, the boys' locker room has open showers, which has been the typical design for years, but the girls' locker room has single shower stalls with curtains. Your husband never had this protection, and when a boy doesn't develop as fast as his peers, he can't hide. He's going to be ridiculed, and that hurts. I know a 46-year-old man who still

> *Boys learn early that competition is the name of the game.*

vividly recalls getting hung by his underwear on the flagpole outside his junior high.

Not only are boys often underdeveloped, but some of us are just plain stupid. In my much younger years, I was eating spaghetti at my mom's friend's house when I passed on the sauce in favor of the butter.

"Kevin," my mom's friend said, "you should have some sauce. It'll put hair on your chest."

That was all I needed to hear. I piled enough sauce on top of those noodles to drown a small rat!

That night, after I got ready for bed, I pulled back my pajamas just as my mom walked into the room.

"Kevin, what are you doing?"

"I'm looking for the hair."

When I explained, my mom had a great laugh, but I was humiliated.

Preadolescence is a tough time for boys. If your husband was the typical boy, he received neither affection nor respect. He was too big to be cuddled in public but too small to be respected by those just slightly older than he was.

Many adult men I meet today still carry shame and guilt about how they "underperformed" as boys. Since many of them grew up in an age when learning disabilities were not recognized as such, they have grown up feeling just plain dumb and often act reserved, because they've learned it's better to be quiet and to be left alone than to speak up and be laughed at.

Why Does My Husband Act Like . . . a Man?

One of my funniest moments as a therapist occurred when a woman started complaining to me about her husband. "I just don't understand him," she said, describing many perfectly normal male traits. "Why does my husband act so much like . . . like . . ."

"A man?" I suggested.

"That's it!"

If you're a woman who, like this one, never had any brothers, your husband is likely a complete mystery to you at times. So let's clear up the mystery a little. Boys are uncomplicated. They're competitive, they do goofy things, and they play rough. And they grow up to be men who are competitive, do goofy things, and play rough.

They're Competitive

While girls huddle in groups on the playground and discuss who's popular and other such topics, the boys argue about who won the last competition. By nature, boys are competitive. They want to win. It doesn't matter whether they're playing a game of Monopoly, tossing around a basketball, or trying to stomp on and kill the highest number of ants. They want to be the best. When they grow up and have a driver's license, they naturally begin counting the number of cars they pass on the way to work. They also compare salaries and the sizes of their offices. Males never really stop competing.

Why does your husband not stop to ask for directions when he's lost (and you're in the car with him)?

A. It's beneath him.
B. He loves to solve things.

C. It's too unmanly to ask for help.

D. He doesn't want any of those cars or trucks he worked so hard to pass to get by him.

All these things might be true of your man to a certain degree, but the best answer is . . . D! With boys and men, competition is the name of the game.

Young coaches quickly catch on to this competitive nature. It's one thing to give a boys' sports team a drill, but if you want to ratchet up the intensity, make the drill competitive—put half of the team against the other half. *Then* you'll see the boys give their best.

A city in the Pacific Northwest decided competition among younger boys was a "bad influence," so the coaches decided to stop keeping score at baseball games. They asked the boys to play their best, and then afterward, when the boys asked who won, they were told, "It doesn't matter as long as you played your hardest."

The experiment never worked because many of the boys kept score anyway. They cared about winning and losing—and why shouldn't they? One of the most important lessons in life is learning how to lose, get up, and keep going. Many of these same boys will be applying for jobs where only 1 out of 10 or even 1 out of 1,000 people will be chosen. They need to learn how to compete, do their best, and face either the pleasure of accomplishment or the pain of falling short.

Competition is one reason that Xbox Online is so wildly popular with boys. The competitive nature of boys is such that brothers will fight to the death over unsolvable disputes—who gets the last piece of pie or whether or not the last runner was tagged out in a game of baseball. Your husband grew up in this world, always fighting for his fair share.

I heard of one hilarious—and typically male—incident when a mother caught her two boys arguing over who would get the first pancake. The mother thought she had a golden opportunity to provide a moral lesson, so she said, "If Jesus were sitting here, he would say, 'Let my brother have the first pancake. I can wait.'" The older son turned to his brother and said, "Okay, Ryan, you be Jesus."

They Do Goofy Things

I can't count the number of stupid things I did as a kid. Even more, I craved the attention that doing goofy things—like eating Milk-Bone dog biscuits—brought me. And my wife tells me that nothing has changed to this day. I guess she's right. She gets a regular dose of the goofiness of boys every time I'm around my buddy Moonhead.

Here's what I mean. Every year Williamsville Central Schools in New York inducts people who have distinguished themselves in their careers to their "Wall of Fame." One year I was given that honor.

Now, there's something you need to know. All of us have miracles in our lives. I'm a walking miracle—there's no two ways about it. I graduated fourth from the bottom of my class in high school. I was in a reading group with a girl who ate paste. My high school counselor, with good reason and just cause, told me in April of my senior year, "Leman, with your grades and record, I couldn't get you admitted to reform school." Yet all these years later, I have my doctorate. And an even greater miracle, I met my wife while I was a janitor.

> *I can't count the number of stupid things I did as a kid. And my wife tells me that nothing has changed to this day.*

So picture me back at my old high school six years ago. Some of my old teachers were still there. I'm sure they would have loved to see me hanging there on a rope. (Let's just say my antics were not appreciated when I was in school.)

What made it more special was that my mom—who had always been my champion, always believing I'd be something even when I was a screwup—was in her ninetieth year. I got to take her with me. At last, for a few minutes, my mother saw her son in high school when she could be really proud of him for something. It took a lot of years, but it finally happened.

Anyway, during the ceremony, the high schoolers were exceptionally well behaved for high schoolers. (Believe me, I've been in a lot of high schools where the kids are rowdy and disrespectful; these kids were great.) When it came time for my award, I got up from my chair to receive it and began to walk across the stage.

Someone yelled out, "Hey, Socks!"

You see, I always wear wild socks. Whenever I'm on TV, you can catch me in shocking pink-and-white-striped socks, or red-and-white checkered socks, or maybe even socks with M&M's on them. It's sort of my thing.

Well, when the principal of the school heard this, he was embarrassed. Immediately he admonished the kids in the most patronizing of tones. He reminded them of their status as the Billies of Williamsville South and that the school had always prided themselves on being a cut above all the others.

But I knew something the principal didn't. Guess who had yelled out, "Hey, Socks"? It *was* a kid from the high school—but one who'd graduated when I did. It was none other than my 59-year-old buddy Moonhead, who was sitting in the audience with his wife, my wife, and my sister.

Women Talk

My husband is a football nut, and I resented that for years. The team in our city isn't even very good (they're perennially one of the worst teams in the NFL), and he'd spend hours watching them play. I couldn't understand the draw.

Then I heard you speak about what's important to men and got a new perspective. With my own money that I'd saved up for something special, I bought my husband the "NFL Ticket"—you know, where you get to see every NFL game on cable. His response? WOW. He loved getting to see every game of his favorite hometown team. When I made the decision to do that and to stop nagging him about watching football all the time, guess what he started doing? Folding the laundry while he watches the game! Those results I'd never have guessed.

Tammy, Virginia

After the presentation, we went to get a bite to eat. We were laughing and hollering over his "Hey, Socks!" comment. Our wives were shaking their heads.

You see, one of my pet phrases is true: the little boy or girl you once were, you still are. I'm not sure that men really grow up even when they're on Medicare. In fact, research shows that women tend to love a sense of humor in a man (I'm sure glad my Sande does!)—that's one of the real drawing points in attracting a woman to a man.

When even grown-up men get together, they get playful. They act like 4-year-olds.

So there I was, just having received a Distinguished Alumni award, and Moonhead and I—both of us in our fifties—started to wrestle in the cafeteria line. Moonhead put me in a headlock. It was a good thing the little old blue heads behind us didn't have cell phones, or they probably would have called 9-1-1. Moonhead and I were play wrestling like two otters next to a stream, but in this case, we were 240-pound otters.

I could tell what our wives were thinking. *Oh, here they go again.*

Some wives would be saying, "Why don't you two just grow up?" But our wives know better. They just let us continue. You see, they realize that we're simple guys at heart and we're playful. That's just a part of who we are.

At our table they even let us continue insulting each other, as men who like each other do.

"Hey, fat boy, what you gonna eat?" Moonhead asked me.

"Well, larger-than-most, I'm thinking of having the chicken parmesan."

I could just see the concerned and shocked looks aimed at us from the next table. *What is wrong with these people?*

Now, I ask you, do you really want your husband to act his age? If so, here's what you'd hear: "My knees are killing me. My back hurts, and my right foot a little . . . or maybe it's my left foot." Wouldn't you rather we provide you a little entertainment, even if it's boy-goofy humor?

They Play Rough

I used to call my big brother "God." That was my nickname for him because that's the way he acted—as if he were accountable to no one but himself. He would walk through the door and I'd call out, "God's home."

My brother regularly pummeled me on a whim. I don't believe he was atypical. Males are far more likely to release their tension by using their fists. That means your husband probably falls into one of two categories: he was beaten up, or he beat someone else up.

A scar on my finger reminds me of the rough-and-tumble world of being a boy. I got the scar from Jimmy's teeth. Jimmy, a neighborhood kid, had the gall to say, "Your mom doesn't love you. Otherwise she'd make you change out of your school clothes before you played." In the next 60 seconds, Jimmy found out just how much my mother loved me, and his mother got to show *her* love by wiping the blood off Jimmy's nose and mouth.

You need to understand the world your husband grew up in. Boys can be extremely cruel to each other. On one occasion, my classmates and I tore the pants off a boy and gave him a "cherry belly" (we slapped his stomach until it turned pink). Then we made him walk through a stretch of itch weed (remember, he wasn't wearing any pants) and forced him to climb a tree—in the nude. This may seem extreme to you if you haven't grown up with boys, but this is what boys do.

> *If you want to have a fascinating conversation with your husband, just ask him about childhood pranks.*

Husbands can get in an occasional tussle with other guys too, but the fights tend to be more verbal. Just like schoolyard boys can make each other's noses bleed and then be best friends ten minutes later, we men can vehemently disagree over an issue, come to an agreement, then shake hands and go play a round of golf—without seeing anything strange about the progression of events.

If you want to have a fascinating conversation with your husband, just ask him about childhood pranks. Then listen carefully to what he says. Was he the one who was beaten up, or the one who was beating someone else up? How does that personality transfer to his actions now, as a man, both at home and what you know of him in the workplace?

How Important His Mama Was Then—and Is Now

If you want to know about your man, look at his mama. Was his mom comfortable with boys?

For your sake, I hope your husband's mom affirmed his maleness. I hope his mom told him what she appreciated about his dad and encouraged the masculine qualities she wanted her son to emulate. In today's world, some moms are more concerned with increasing a male's sensitivity toward the female population than with affirming male qualities. But such tactics don't produce tolerance or increased sensitivity toward the female population. Instead, they create confusion—and confused kids tend to make terrible, traumatic choices.

Is it okay for boys to do "girly" things? Sure. If a boy has an older sister, it's only natural that, for instance, he will sometimes play with dolls. One of my early childhood memories is of playing paper dolls with my sister, Sally. She was older than I was, so when I drifted into her world, we played what she wanted to play. She certainly never asked me, "What do *you* want to do, Kevin?" Since she was older, I had to be on her terms if I wanted to play with her, so that meant playing with dolls.

If your husband grew up with all sisters, he's probably very comfortable in the world of girls. But there's a huge difference between being comfortable *with* girls and always wanting to act *like* a girl.

Males who grow up to be mature adults have usually benefited from clearly defined gender roles. I've never seen a confused kid make consistently good life choices. He'd better get his identity figured out before he gets married, or he and his wife will suffer accordingly. I can't tell you how many struggling couples I've counseled where the husband is actually a gay man hiding behind the guise of marriage. No wonder there's no glue, no sizzle, to the marriage.

Although you may think it's your husband's *father* who formed who his son became, his *mother* is the one who probably had a greater impact on him—and she directly influenced how your husband treats you now.

The Overprotective Mother

You can control a 3-year-old, but you can't ultimately control a 12-year-old. You can guide a child, but the opportunity to control a child at that age is extremely limited.

Your husband probably realized this before his mother did. He figured out that he could lie and get away with it, that he was smart enough to occasionally sneak out of the house, and that it was possible to hide the smell of cigarette smoke if he gave it some careful thought.

In this dawning of manhood, your husband's attitude toward women either took a giant step forward into maturity, or it was frozen into a glacier of disrespect. Particularly because boys are so competitive, an overprotective mothering style is a prescription for disaster. The smother mother won't let her boy do anything that might cause him to get hurt. No sports, no climbing trees, no going on hikes—in short, all the things boys love most. So what happens when he gets out from under her thumb? He has an "I'll show you" attitude and proceeds to present it to the world. Such "bad boys" can seem attractive while you're dating—because of the adventure, excitement, and danger—but look out if you're married to one.

> **What to Do on Tuesday**
>
> 1. Observe your male creature in his environment. In what setting does he seem most comfortable? Why do you think that is?
> 2. What were his growing-up years like?
> 3. How did his mother interact with him? How did his father treat his mother?
> 4. In what way(s) does his background contribute to who he is now, and how he responds to you and life in general?
> 5. Was he encouraged to share his feelings?

Unfortunately, if his mama was a weak-willed woman—always picking up after her son, always lying to cover for him—he's going to expect that you, his wife, will be the same. So what he couldn't dish out to his mama while he was under her thumb, he's going to dish out to you.

When a boy learns early on that he can control and manipulate his mother, he'll assume he can do the same to you. If you're a pleaser, you're likely to fall under his control rather than stand up and say no.

Ask Dr. Leman

Q: I used to be an accountant before I got married and had kids. We didn't want anyone else raising our kids, so we made the joint decision that I'd stay home with them. But now my husband is always talking about "his money," as opposed to "our money." I'm a careful spender. I even clip coupons and save our family a couple hundred bucks a month. He questions everything I spend and wants me to account for every penny I spend at the grocery store. I hate it. How can I get him to stop?

Janice, New Mexico

A: Here's what I'd do, Janice. I wouldn't set foot in a grocery store for a long time. You're not a servant, and he's not lord over your money. When he wonders why his dinner is just lettuce and croutons, tell him straight out, "Because that's what we have left in the house." Then tell him that you really hate having to wrestle money out of him. (For goodness' sake, you used to be an accountant; I think you know the value of money.) Say, "I don't enjoy feeling like I'm some servant and you're the lord of the manor. I don't want to feel that way again. So I've decided that you can do the shopping for a while." Hand him the envelope of clipped coupons, then make a graceful exit out of the room. I bet his jaw will drop to the floor behind you.

When he tries to get you to shop, say a firm no. If he's going to complain about giving you money to shop, he needs to do it for himself to see how good of a shopper you really are. Sure, you may have strange meals for a while. But I would bet you one of my prized jukeboxes that after a couple weeks of having to shop for the groceries himself, that man will hand you back the coupons along with some cash (and probably more than he's given you before). And there won't be any more complaints either. Bon appétit!

The No-Room-to-Fail Mama

Did your husband's mother give him any room to fail, or did she expect him to be perfect? Did she tell him to make his bed, inspect it, and then remake it so it was perfect? Was she always bossing him around and telling him what to do?

If so, then your husband is likely to react negatively and often explosively to any criticism of yours. You might think it's a minor thing to point out that the mirror he hung is a bit crooked, but what does he hear in his head? *You've messed up. You're an absolute failure. I knew you couldn't do anything right!* You don't mean to convey this impression, but because of his rearing, that's exactly what your husband hears. In the male mind, there are no degrees of success—only pass or fail.

So what do you do? Just not say anything? Well now, that wouldn't accomplish much, would it?

There's a better way to take the tension out of such a situation: brag about your husband to his face! Let him know that you appreciate the character qualities his mother might have missed, and that despite some of his shortcomings, you're delighted with your catch.

Will such words make a change overnight, or even by the end of the week? Probably not. Remember that you are combating at least 18 years of his mother's negative training, so it will take a while.

How would this work with the crooked mirror? You could say, "That looks terrific, honey. You put the mirror exactly where I want it. It's so good of you to get that done. I wonder, however, if it's a little crooked. Do you think that's a problem, or is it just me?"

Trust me, that man will take another look at that mirror, and he'll use his logical, analytical mind to adjust it perfectly to your liking—without being colored by the emotions his mother invoked in him.

The Driven Mother

Do you ever wonder why your husband can't slow down? Why he always has to keep moving, keep working, and even play hard as if he's working?

It probably has everything to do with how he was reared. Did his mother keep him busy, busy, busy? Did she pack his after-school hours and weekends with scheduled events—especially events where he had to perform? Did she hold high expectations for everything he did, both at home and at school? Was he allowed any downtime where he could choose what he wanted to do? Did his family focus on togetherness, or did the family members go their separate ways during dinner or vacation times?

If your husband grew up in a home with a driven mother, he may not really have bonded with his family. He may not be used to being together, because he was never really together with his family in his growing-up years. If your husband was programmed to be driven, you have a lifelong battle getting him to slow down. But you can help him do it, by degrees. This one won't be fixed by Friday, but you can certainly take a crack at it by adjusting your own activities. Also, tell your husband how important he is and his presence is to your family, and that you miss him when he's not there. Plan vacations as a family. Set aside a couple nights a week, for starters, to make "just the family" dinners, and cook something special.

Your husband needs you to save him from himself and the program running in his head. Otherwise he'll run himself ragged. So help him put on the brakes, slowly and gently. Showing him that you respect him, need him, and want to fulfill him will go a long way toward keeping that man at home and in the family court.

The Disciplining Mother

This mama knows the way to do it. When the kids act up, she's not the one who says, "Wait until your father gets home." Instead she says, "We need to talk right now. I won't put up with that. You know better, and I'm not going to let you get away with that."

Her kids think she's tough sometimes, but she's always fair. When she says that something will happen, it does. Promised consequences follow actions. If Andy doesn't take out the trash, then she simply doesn't take him to his friend's to play that night, and Andy has to call his friend and explain why.

> *Your husband needs you to save him from himself and the program running in his head.*

The disciplining mother doesn't do anything for the child that he can do for himself. She wants him to be strong and self-sufficient. She insists that he pull his weight around the house and fulfill his list of chores. Yet she is tender and loving toward her child as well.

If you married a man with this type of mother, then you most likely have a great and attentive husband on your hands, who understands the consequences of his actions and knows that you're not a pushover. Because he had respect for his mother, he's likely to have respect for you.

You can't compete with a mother's upbringing. But you can work around it. If you married a man with issues, you have a job ahead of you. If you didn't, be incredibly thankful—and make sure to thank your mother-in-law!

What He Longs For

Today your grown-up boy longs for the same things from you that he longed for from his mama (and may or may not have received): acceptance, belonging, and companionship.

He needs to know that he has your unconditional acceptance. That even if he loses his job in a rough economy, you won't think less of him. That he'll still be your man, your lover, your provider. The one you'd choose to marry all over again.

He also needs to feel that he belongs to you. Quite frankly, your husband doesn't have anything else to really belong to. Sure, he goes to work, but he doesn't belong there. He may work out at a gym or play basketball on Thursday nights with the guys, but he doesn't belong to them. He only has himself—and you. Those guys who have one good male friend are truly blessed.

Now, you take your husband, then add a job, a busy life, and several kids to the mix. You tell me where your man fits into that paradigm. Does your guy know that he belongs to the family? That he's needed? That his role as husband and daddy are important, and that you can't imagine life without him?

The ABCs Every Man Needs

Acceptance
Belonging
Companionship

He needs your companionship. You, and only you, are at the top of his "want to spend time with" list. It may seem like his buddies are on top, or that work priorities override you, but that simply isn't true. But it is true that if you show that you're too busy to include him in your life, he'll find other things to replace his time. Underneath it all, though, his little-boy heart is crying, *But what about me? Where do I fit on your to-do list? Don't I matter?*

How you as a wife answer those unspoken longings has everything to do with the kind of husband your man will be by Friday.

Predictable Is His Middle Name

We men are pretty predictable creatures. That can have its pluses and its minuses. On the plus side, we can be good, consistent providers. We don't wander off (you usually have a good idea of where we are). On the minus side, we can be boring because we're afraid of taking any risks or making any changes.

There's an old joke about a guy who worked on high-rise buildings in New York. For four days his co-workers watched him open his lunchbox, and the same thing would happen every day. He'd say, "Ham and cheese—again," and slam his lunchbox shut with disgust. When the fifth day rolled around, again the guy opened his lunchbox, peered in, and said with disgust, "Oh no. Ham and cheese again. I'm so sick and tired of ham and cheese."

The worker sitting next to him leaned over and said, "Hey, it's none of my business, but why don't you tell your wife you're sick and tired of ham and cheese and you want something else?"

The guy looked shocked. "Hey, buddy!" he retorted. "I make my own sandwich!"

Your husband is a little like a bobcat. He'll walk the same path over and over and over again. He has a route he's used to, and he'll follow it.

If someone said, "Hey, Kevin, if we went to Red Lobster, what would you have?" I'd tell him straight up, "The coconut shrimp." I order the same thing all the time. (And yes, there are a few Renaissance men who will try new things, but I don't happen to be one of them very often.) I don't even need the menu, I'm so predictable.

> *Your husband is a little like a bobcat. He'll walk the same path over and over and over again. He has a route he's used to, and he'll follow it.*

Then there's Sande, who looks at what's on the tables all around us and says, "What's that man having over there? Mmm, that looks good. Maybe I'll try that."

When we men are sick, we're also predictable. We whine, we act like we're at death's door—when all we have is a cold. We just need a little babying sometimes.

72

Now you women? You can have a sore throat, a cold, the flu, and a 102-degree temp, and still be running the kids to school and then be off to work. Nothing that a little DayQuil can't cure, is there?

The key to understanding what your man really needs is easy because he's so predictable. It's what he grouses about. "I don't get any respect around here. . . . No one listens to me." Do you know what he's really saying with such complaining comments? "Hey! Don't I matter around here? Aren't I good for something?"

Because you are so good at multitasking and seem to do everything so perfectly, if your guy isn't helping you around the house, it could be because he thinks you don't need or want his help. Every husband wants to be trusted.

Have you ever had someone leaning over your shoulder, trying to read the same newspaper, magazine, or book you're reading? Does that bother you? It annoys most people. It will annoy your husband too, if he wants to help or agrees to help with a project, when you're always looking over his shoulder. "Uh, not that way. Try it this way. . . . If you just did X, that would work better."

No self-respecting guy wants to be *told* what to do, like you're his mama. You're his wife, his partner, not the commandant of his projects. If you're the helicopter wife hovering over him, he's going to throw down whatever he's helping you with and say, "Well, why don't you just do it?" and stalk off, because he doesn't like to be micromanaged. (Think about it: do you?)

Men will get the job done, but they might not necessarily do it the way you would. But is that wrong, or just different?

One Saturday morning, when our oldest daughter, Holly, was a baby, I told Sande to go ahead and take the day to do something fun with a girlfriend. "Honey, don't worry about a thing," I said, meaning every word of it. So off Sande went for a needed respite.

Within a few minutes, Holly messed her pants beyond belief. It was a #2 to beat all. In those days it was real cloth diapers. No

Pampers. So what did I do? The plan made perfect sense to me. I took her out in the backyard, got the garden hose out, and hosed her off.

I got away with it for a few days . . . until Holly told her mama about the special bath she'd had in the backyard. But I got the job done, didn't I?

Your guy will get the job done, but in man style. And if you look over his shoulder and tell him how to do it differently, he takes that as, *You don't trust me to get the job done, do you? I'm not that incompetent!* And then your help around the house disappears, because he doesn't want to risk your criticism again.

Your husband's a simple guy, but don't mistake that for simpleminded (although you may wonder at times). The simplicity of a man is that he sees things in lockstep, linear fashion. And he knows when he's being had, when he's being suckered, when he's being taken advantage of. Believe me.

When men don't feel respected and trusted, most will shut down. They'll get quiet and make all kinds of assumptions, such as, *You don't really love me. If you really loved me, you wouldn't correct me. You wouldn't hang me out to dry in front of your girlfriends like that.* Some men will explode and make fools of themselves. It has so much to do with background.

A Husband's Deadly Sins

Using good towels to clean the car.
Walking with muddy shoes on your just-cleaned kitchen floor.
Making a mess.
Making a mess, then not picking up after himself.
Leaving newspapers lying around.
Bringing someone home for dinner without calling first.
Saying his mother-in-law looks hot in a bathing suit.
Commenting on your weight.
Telling you, "I like your hair"—when you got it cut nine weeks ago.

Give Him a Little Credit

Remember when I said that boys' brains have much less sensory awareness than girls' brains? Well, the same is true of men. One career woman in her early forties—I'll call her Sue—came to see me because she was so frustrated with her husband's amazing ability to live with debris. She came from a neatnik home, and it was driving her crazy.

One morning she noticed that there was an empty toilet paper roll lying on the floor in one section of the master bathroom (which was only six feet by six feet). She decided to conduct an experiment. She dated the toilet paper roll and placed it back exactly where she'd found it. She wanted to see how long it would take her husband, Craig, to pick it up. After all, picking up after him wasn't her job. He wasn't a child—or was he?

An entire week went by, and every morning Sue checked the bathroom and discovered that the toilet paper roll was still there, lying on the floor. A month went by, two months, three months, then four months—an entire season! Sue had found the toilet paper roll at the end of October, and it was now the end of February.

Finally she couldn't take it anymore. When Craig came home from work, she walked him into the bathroom and told him, "I've been conducting a test. Do you have any idea what the test might be?"

Craig looked around. "You didn't paint the walls, did you?"

"No."

"The floor's the same, isn't it?"

"Yes."

"I'm sorry, I—"

She lost her cool and snapped, "The toilet paper roll! Didn't you notice it on the floor? Look, I dated it—October 30. It's been lying here for four months!"

Craig shrugged. "I'm sorry. I guess I just didn't see it."

And when I asked him about it, he honestly hadn't! That's because when he went into the bathroom, he was focusing on getting one job done, and only one. He wasn't noticing everything else in the periphery of his vision. But if Sue had said, "Hey, honey, would you mind picking up the toilet paper rolls from the floor when you change them? I'd really appreciate it," then picking up that roll would have been on his radar. And it would have saved four months of stress on Sue's part.

Wendy, a stay-at-home mom with an at-home business, conducted a test of her own. It was driving her crazy that her husband, Allen, acted like she was the only one who could buy toothpaste. One time she watched Allen squeeze and squeeze a virtually empty tube, wondering when he'd get the clue and drive down to Walgreens to pick some up on his own.

That never happened. Instead, Allen came downstairs one evening and said, "Wendy? I can't get any more toothpaste out of the tube, and the boys need to brush their teeth. Do we have a new tube?"

If you wait for your guy to notice you need something, you'll be waiting a long time.

"I don't know," Wendy said. "Have you bought any lately?"

Allen was about as perplexed as a husband could be. "No." He laughed, as if buying toothpaste was the most bizarre thing he could imagine doing.

"Well, then, I guess we're out," Wendy replied.

Now, Allen might be simple, but he wasn't simpleminded. He could tell by her tone that something was up, so he said, "How about if I go buy some?"

"That's a great idea," Wendy said, thinking, *Well, well, it's about time. He's finally getting it!*

At least, she thought it was a great idea until he came home with, in her words, "Galactic Blue Bubblemint Star Wars Toothpaste!"

I have to confess that, as a man, I sat stumped in my therapist's chair. I wasn't sure what the problem was. After all, she'd wanted Allen to buy the toothpaste, didn't she?

"Have you ever had to clean that stuff up?" Wendy half yelled at me in reply, as if I was simpleminded. "That blue gunk sticks to everything!"

When Wendy bought toothpaste, she thought, *What toothpaste will make the least mess?* When Allen bought toothpaste, he thought, *What toothpaste will make the kids the happiest?*

It was a simple misunderstanding—the kind that happens in every marriage. It's part of the great gap that exists between what a woman values and what a man values. But if you're going to understand this creature you've married, you're going to need to give him a little credit. Wendy could have saved herself a lot of aggravation if she would have just told Allen, "On your way home tonight, would you pick up some Crest toothpaste at Walgreens? We're out, and I can't get that errand done today. I'd really appreciate it." What do you think that guy would arrive home with? Crest toothpaste. He has his assignment, it's specific (so he knows exactly what to get), and she's telling him he's needed and appreciated.

Now, isn't that a better way to go? Like with Craig and the toilet paper roll, if you wait for your guy to notice you need something, you'll be waiting a long time. Why not simply ask?

If you make a little effort, it'll pay back tenfold. I guarantee it, because I see it happen all the time.

When you catch him doing something right, reinforce that. Tell him how much you appreciate it. Brag about him in front of your friends. "Do you know what my sweet Roger did? I've been working overtime on this big project and got home late, and he'd made us a lasagna. I didn't even know he knew how to make lasagna. And he'd already cleaned up the kitchen too. I could have cried, I was so happy." Even better, brag about him in front of your friends when he's in the room. He'll be puffing up inside, thinking, *I'm the man.*

Ask Dr. Leman

Q: I have a husband, two teenagers, and a really intense job where I have to travel. Every time I get home from a trip, I walk into the house and it's a mess. It takes me half a day to clean it up. And no one's there volunteering to help out, that's for sure. Mark says, "I'm so glad you're home!" and retreats behind his newspaper. Can he not see the pizza cartons and crud all over the kitchen counter?

Exasperated in Omaha

A: Well, Exasperated in Omaha, I can see why you're exasperated. No one likes coming home to a mess, and you're not put on this earth to be a slave dog.

But have you ever thought about it this way? Does your husband really *see* that mess? Does it bother him like it bothers you? Most likely not. He doesn't mean to exasperate you; he just has different priorities. Why not tell Mark, "It's hard for me to come home and find the house a mess. Do you think you and the kids could clean up next time before I come home?" Chances are that a lightbulb will pop on in your husband's head, and he'll think, *What a great idea. Why didn't I think of that?* Try it out and see what happens.

A month later . . .

Dr. Leman,

I can't believe it. I just got home from a trip, and the entire house was sparkling clean—even the kitchen. No pizza boxes in sight. It even looked like someone dusted. Blow me over. No one dusts anymore. It had to be Mark, because the kids are away on a school trip and aren't returning until tonight. Wow. Your advice really works!

Dear E-i-O,

Glad you think so. Let me give you some more. Now that you have Marky boy right where you want him, reinforce that behavior. He really does want to please you. So when he gets home tonight, why not give him a pleasant surprise? Tell him, "You know, I really appreciated you cleaning up the house. It looks awesome." Then take him back to the bedroom, bolt the door in case the kids get home early, and have a wonderful sexual interlude with him. That's the way to slip a commercial to him that says, "I **love** it when you do things like this for me. It makes me feel like making love to you. I'm so glad I married a man like you." That boy will be eating out of your hand, and you'll have the cleanest house around!

It's All about Consequences

Sometimes your guy needs to experience some consequences. Take helping out around the house, for instance. Most men don't help out around the house. They don't cook, clean, or grocery shop. They drop their clothes right where they take them off. All those things are a woman's domain, such guys think. But they're wrong. Being a family means that everyone helps out with whatever needs to get done.

Women Talk

I did what you said. I stood up for myself and let my husband experience the consequences. Here's what happened. One day I decided to make his favorite—baby-back ribs—for dinner, but I didn't have any barbecue sauce. We have only one car, so I called him at work and said, "Would you do me a big favor and stop at the store on your way home?"

He said, "No, I can't. I'm too busy," and hung up on me.

I was really hurt, to put it bluntly. Here I'd gone out of my way to make his favorite, and he couldn't even help me out with a five-minute run to the grocery store. But instead of getting mad or getting even, like I usually do, I remembered what you said and let the consequences play out.

That night he was whining like a stuck pig at dinner. "Where's the barbecue sauce? You can't have baby-back ribs without barbecue sauce."

I calmly said, "Earlier today, if you remember, I called you and asked you to stop at the store. I have no way of getting to the store without a car. But you said you were too busy. I needed you to pick up only one thing: barbecue sauce."

I could tell by the look on his face that he got it. He ate the ribs without any more complaints (that's a first too; he always complains nonstop about what I make for dinner).

*That was a month ago. Since then I've called him only once to ask him to get something at the store, and he said, "Sure, no problem." Then yesterday, he called **on his way home** from work and asked if I needed anything. Can you believe that? Well, I guess you can, since you told me that's what would happen.*

I didn't think my husband could change. But the consequence thing really works. Next I'm going to try it on my kids!

Pamela, Mississippi

When your husband doesn't help out, you don't need to put him down. You don't need to make a mountain out of a molehill. You just need to train him. People train puppies, so why can't you train your husband? Men are trainable, and the best way for them to learn is through consequences.

For example, let's say you're sick of doing everything around the house. The house could be a pigsty, and he wouldn't care. Sure, you can pick up after him to make a point and then wag your finger in his face when you see him. "Look what I had to clean up. It's your mess, but no, I'm the one who had to do it. You never help. You always make a mess. . . ." You know what he hears after he sees you standing there with your hands on your hips? "Blah, blah, blah." Your words don't even enter the computer between his ears.

But what if you tried this simple scheme: What if you didn't pick up the stuff he lets lay around? What if someone stops by to see him unexpectedly and sees the family room trashed, and he's embarrassed? So? Will that kill him? No, but it will teach him a valuable lesson about consequences.

If he forgets to take the garbage out on Monday and it stays in the garage next to his prized Corvette, so? Don't take it out yourself. Let it stay there and stink up his territory. I bet you anything he'll remember it next Monday.

After all, men are trainable.

Cut Him Some Slack

Before you get frustrated with your male, remember that guys in general are clueless about relationships. Sometimes I'm dumb as mud (just ask my wife), and I have a doctorate degree. Instead of expecting your husband to read your mind, be specific about what you want him to do. Clue him in on what's important to you. I guarantee you, if you say it in a nice way, he'll be grateful. You're a natural wordsmith, so I know you can do a good job at that.

But just remember, your words have to match your behavior. You can say all the nice words you want, but if he doesn't feel respected by your actions, you might as well go out and try to talk to the tree in your backyard.

There's an old saying: before you judge someone, it's good to walk a mile in their shoes. We men might not be very relational, but we get a lot of psychological fulfillment from providing for our families, even if we feel the pressure of it every day. But it's far more emotionally fulfilling to have the provision *recognized*. Inside every man is the little boy who wants to hear "Good job!" from you.

So the next time you see your husband, give him a tremendous gift that won't cost you a dime: tell him, "Thanks so much for . . ." and list three or four things you typically take for granted.

If you want to have a new husband by Friday:

Talk to him with gentleness, kindness, and respect.

Show him in both words and actions that you accept him, that he belongs to your family, and that you believe he's competent.

Honor him in your home. Ask him what he thinks.

Be efficient and independent, but not too much; he needs to be needed.

Tell him what's going on in the family; he likes to know what's going on, even if he can't be there all the time. Every man hates finding out information about his family thirdhand.

Show an interest in what he likes to do.

Listen to him (when he does talk).

If you do those things, you'll have a man who will be a one-woman man for life, will enjoy providing for you, and will provide for you well. He'll be a happy dude. He'll do anything to please you. And after all, isn't that what you want in your new husband by Friday?

BONUS SECTION

What do you do with a man who is critical, disrespectful, or abusive?

There are men who use their wives, who take advantage of them. But you don't have to put up with it.

This section is for those who've had enough, and for those who've been beaten down.

AIN'T GOT NO RESPECT

This morning I did a radio show. A 23-year-old woman called in with a question. She was the mother of a 7-year-old and a 3-month-old. She wasn't married; she was living with a guy. She was paying all the bills; he wasn't doing anything but sitting around. "All he does is criticize me," she said. She was cook, bottle washer, housemaid, and sex partner, and that man didn't do a lick to contribute to the relationship. He was using her.

"Dump the chump," I said vehemently. "You have your whole life ahead of you, and that guy doesn't deserve to be part of it."

But when you're married, it's not quite that easy to rid yourself of a rough relationship, is it?

You picked up this book for a reason. Deep in your heart you know you need a new husband because the one you have isn't a husband. He's a man you're married to who controls you, doesn't respect you, doesn't listen to you, yells at you, and might even knock you around. He cheats, he lies, he's dishonest to the core, he's a womanizer, and he's a whole lot of other things. None of them are things you want in a man.

I want to be clear up front. In these situations, there's no magic dust you can sprinkle over the relationship and have that white picket fence pop up around your house. That's not realistic; that's not how life is. The reality is that many people marry exactly the wrong person. People who don't feel good about themselves and don't have a healthy picture of themselves will gravitate toward people who aren't good for them. It's no wonder that more than half of today's couples get divorced.

> *The reality is that most people marry exactly the wrong person.*

If you're thinking about divorce as an option, here are some things to consider in your decision. What do your state's divorce laws say about health benefits, retirement benefits, portions of his income that would be yours, child custody, etc.? If you have a job, would your income alone cover your living expenses (house, car, etc.)? How would you make any additional income to cover your expenses and put away a little nest egg for the future? (Would you go back to school, come up with creative options for day care?) Do you have a shared checking and savings account, with both you and your husband as cosigners, or is your husband's name the only one on the account? Where would you live? Would you be able to afford staying in your house, if that's an option? At what age and stage are your children (if any), and how would they respond to Mommy and Daddy living apart? How would you want to handle child custody, including holidays? Where would your children go to school?

Gathering the information about these questions and others is extremely important. In situations of abuse (physical, sexual, emotional, and verbal), marriage cannot and does not work long term. You should not, and cannot, put up with abuse of any kind in your home.

But divorce is not the easy, instant fix that many think it will be. There are long-term effects for everyone involved. Considering those effects will help you make a careful, informed choice for your own welfare and your children's welfare.

Ask Dr. Leman

Q: My husband has been cheating on me for over eight years with an employee from work. I've known about it all along but put up with it because we have two kids, and I didn't want them to be without a father. But he's not around much; I'm the one who cooks dinner and helps them with their homework every night. Our daughter isn't doing very well in school. She has a lot of behavioral issues and doesn't respect anyone, the school principal told me.

Now Ted has filed for divorce. Should I fight it? Do you think we can reconcile? Is it worth it?

Patti, New Hampshire

A: Why on earth would you want to reconcile with a man who has been that disrespectful of you and your marriage vows for eight years? Obviously he's not keeping you and the kids in consideration; he's leaving you holding the bag. And all this because he's bringing home a paycheck?

You say you're staying together because of the children. You're not doing your children much of a favor, to tell you the truth. Especially if your kids know what's going on and that you're tolerating it. With a father as a negative role model, no wonder your daughter has behavioral issues and doesn't respect authority. If I were her, I wouldn't either.

Now is the time for you to stand up for yourself—for both your well-being and the kids'. There is no reconciliation here. He left you long ago; now he's just seeking the paperwork. Let the man go, but fight for the finances to keep you and your children afloat.

Let me state this next point very firmly. If I err as a counselor, I err on the side of trying to make things work. Sometimes that

> **Take Back Your Life!**
>
> 1. Stand up for yourself. You're worth it.
> 2. What you think counts, and your ideas count.
> 3. Everyone doesn't have to like what you say and think.
> 4. If you act like you are a person of value, people will respond to you that way.

means slogging through unpleasant stuff to get there. But you are *never* to be some guy's punching bag—physically, sexually, emotionally, or verbally—even if that guy is your husband. If your husband is a philanderer, he abandoned his marriage vows a long time ago. If you are married to an abusive person, you need to stand up for yourself. You need to begin to protect yourself legally and financially. You need to take control of your life for your own safety, and for the emotional and physical safety of your children.

The Apple Doesn't Fall Far from the Tree

Whoever came up with the phrase "the apple doesn't fall far from the tree" was sure a smart cookie. The reality is that when you married, more than two of you walked down that flower-strewn aisle. You got your mom and dad, his mom and dad, and any stepparents along the way too. You didn't get a taco with just meat and cheese; you got lettuce, hot sauce, the refried beans that come back at you, tomatoes, sour cream—the whole enchilada.

Your guy's taco came packed with all the value-added ingredients of the concepts he learned from his family. He caught the disrespectful way his father treated his mother, and guess who he's passing it on to? You. If you looked back and saw your husband's father treat his wife with disrespect and saw your son treat his mother with disrespect, how could you think you would fare any better? That you'd be treated with respect, kindness, affirmation, and courtesy?

"I know, I know," you're saying, "but we were in love, and I thought it would turn out okay." In those euphoric touches of dating, both of you were likely on your best behavior. He might have looked like a purebred to you, but then you got married and found out you had, at best, a Heinz 57 mongrel.

Why am I telling you this now, when it's too late? Because it might not be too late for your next relationship, if there is one, when you consider these important points.

Am I advocating you dump the chump? No, that's not what I'm saying. If children are involved, you have even more to consider. Does that mean you're forever condemned to live in a marriage devoid of respect? Absolutely not. What I am saying is that you cannot allow the disrespect to continue within your marriage. But to change the cycle, you'll need to change the way you relate to your husband.

If you wait for your husband to change, nothing will happen. If you nag him, you'll become even more miserable than he is (and nagging will make him respect you less, because nagging appears to be a weakness). So what can you do?

Remember that your husband is a creature of habit. To get a guy to notice something, you have to break through his normal routine. Since men are predisposed to fix things, sometimes he has to see for himself that something is broken before he'll pay attention to it.

For example, let's say your husband, Frank, comes home from work one afternoon and immediately barks, "Where's my dry cleaning? Why didn't you pick up my dry cleaning?"

You know you can't win this argument, so refuse to get into it. If it really is your fault, apologize for your forgetfulness, then remind yourself that even if you did mess up, you deserve to be treated with respect. And tonight you're going to do something about it.

About an hour and a half later, Frank may notice that there's no dinner on the table. He'll probably scratch his head, go back into the den, and expect that you're just running a little late. But after another thirty minutes, when he doesn't hear anything in the kitchen, he's guaranteed to ask, "Where's dinner?"

Don't blow up. Don't whine. Say in a calm and casual voice, "I don't feel like cooking dinner."

"What do you mean you don't feel like cooking dinner?"

Stay cool. Don't get into an argument. Simply answer, "Well, Frank, you came home two hours ago, snapped at me, and said, 'Where's my dry cleaning?' The fact is, I spent most of the morning cleaning up after the Monday Night Football party you had with your friends, and then your mom called and asked me to come over this afternoon to run some errands for her. I'm sorry I forgot your dry cleaning, but I think I deserve to be treated with a little more respect. When you attack me without even trying to understand what my day was like, it makes me feel that you don't respect me. When I'm not respected, I don't feel like cooking."

Most often a husband doesn't notice when a wife feels demeaned. (It all goes back to the fact that a male has less sensory perception.) So you have to do something to make him see that the relationship is broken. If you just talk at him, you won't accomplish much. (In the next chapter, we'll talk about what you say and how your husband receives it.) But if you create a situation, the chances that your message will get through will increase dramatically.

Women Talk

My husband was majorly taking me for granted. He always criticized me and everything I did. Nothing was ever good enough. And he always threatened to divorce me. Every time he mentioned that, I got really scared because we have three young kids. What would I do? So I'd go out of my way to make him happy . . . until the next blow-up.

Then I took your advice, Dr. Leman. You said it was time for me to take him by surprise—to tell him that I wanted a divorce—to see if that would wake him up to what he was doing. You were right. That stopped him just as he was starting to crank up the criticism again. His jaw dropped, and he just stared at me.

We're now going to counseling together. He told the counselor recently that it was like a bomb went off in his brain, realizing he might lose me and the kids. You were right again: sometimes you have to take the bull by the horns in order to bring about change. Our home is changing—slowly, but it's changing.

Alicia, Washington

Also, you need to take a good, hard look at where your husband came from. How did your husband's dad treat his mom? How did his mom treat his dad? If your husband grew up with a father who was violent toward his wife or emotionally distant, what did your husband learn about marriage? Women? Himself? How did his parents handle curveballs? How did they communicate? By yelling, fighting, then freezing each other out until someone felt guilty and apologized? Did they fight like cats and dogs, yet never get anywhere? Perhaps they held grudges, making the environment tense at home. Problems were never resolved; they were buried and then built up, like plaque on teeth. How have those patterns your husband learned from his parents affected his relationship with you?

It's all about the domino effect. I've learned a lot about that lately in regard to cars and electrical problems. In 60-plus years of walking around this earth, I still know nothing about cars and those things. But I do know that if I'm told I have an electrical problem in my car, it can end up costing me a fortune, because there are so many different ways the problem can manifest itself. In this day of high-tech engines, I can spend a lot of money at the local repair shop, especially at the going rate of 70-plus bucks an hour. I don't want electrical problems; they're hard to track down. Just when I think the problem is in one area, it shows up in another area. It's like looking for the proverbial needle in the haystack.

Everyone is wired differently. Some of those wires are where they should be; others aren't. If they've had no interference over the years and have been dealt with in the proper way, they'll be in good shape and won't cause you problems. But in some environments, those wires were pulled, played with, neglected, or abused. So is it any surprise that over a period of time those mangled wires will come to the forefront and cause problems?

The Pleaser

In marriage, each spouse should try to please the other. But there's a problem when one person is doing all the pleasing and the other is doing all the taking.[2]

A pleaser often looks confident and successful on the outside, but underneath, her private logic tells her that she can never do enough or be enough to make others happy. She is often a perfectionist who was actively influenced by parental pressure. She grew up in a critical, unhappy home, with little fatherly attention, support, or love. In marriage she puts up with the way her husband treats her because she doesn't think she deserves any better treatment. At least, Mom and Dad didn't think so, and they had to be right.

There's a problem when one person is doing all the pleasing and the other is doing all the taking.

A pleaser thinks everything is her fault. If only she'd done something different, if only she'd said something different, then maybe her husband wouldn't have yelled, blown up, and hit her. A pleaser wants the highway of

92

life to be smooth, with no road bumps. "Peace at any price" is her motto. But she's the one who pays dearly. She's the doormat, and everyone (husband included) takes advantage of her. She's valued for what she does (cooking, cleaning, laundry), not for who she is.

Ironically, a pleaser tends to marry a controller or a "dependent loser" who takes advantage of her.

> *A pleaser wants the highway of life to be smooth, with no road bumps. "Peace at any price" is her motto. But she's the one who pays dearly.*

The Controller

A controller grew up watching his father denigrate, harass, and verbally and/or physically abuse his mother, and he developed a philosophy that women are weak and are to be dominated. He'll often repent of his outbursts: "I'm sorry, please forgive me. I won't do it again." The pleaser wife wants to believe it, so she'll tell herself, *He really is sorry. He says he is. I guess I deserved it.* But the same scenario plays out over and over again. The controller gets his psychological jollies by dominating someone who is weaker than him. He might do this physically, verbally, or by controlling the flow of money in the household.

A controller isn't always verbally or physically abusive, however. He can also end up controlling his wife through her pity and desire to help him. This type of man I call the "dependent loser." His wife is a "Martha" Luther—a reformer—who is sure that if she just works hard enough, she can change her man into the guy she wants him to be. But she spends her life walking around her husband on eggshells.

Nipping Control in the Bud

Thousands of men hide from life behind women's skirts. They'll complain about things, like the flat-screen TV they bought that doesn't work right. They'll complain and complain—all behind closed doors. When it comes to talking to the salesperson, that same husband will take the low road. Oftentimes you, the *wife*, are the one who takes the TV back to the store. See what I mean? You need to become good at backing off and allowing your husband to step up to the plate and be a man, not a mouse.

You are not put on this earth to be your husband's doormat or servant.

Is there a guy your husband respects who is a good influence on him? A mentor who could take your male creature under his wings and teach him how to be a good husband? Is there a small group at your place of worship that you could join? Any kind of group that would foster relationships? Would your husband see a professional?

> *You are not put on this earth to be your husband's doormat or servant.*

Your husband's response will tell you a lot about whether he's willing to make a change. If he is, wonderful! Encourage him to pursue that change in every way that you can't. If he's not willing, it might be better to let your marriage go. There will be far more hurt in the long run.

Andrea was married to a high-powered business executive. He was a rat. He slept around and violated his marriage many times. He wasn't a particularly good husband or father. He had just served her with divorce papers when she came to see me. He was determined to take the kids, and he had her over the barrel because he had money and good lawyers. Andrea was absolutely paralyzed at the thought of losing her children and worried about what was going to happen to them.

I finally got her to see that her husband was a controller, and he knew Mama Bear's soft spot—her little cubs. Did he really want the kids? No. What would a jet-setting business executive do with two kids all day? Take them on his business trips? Have them sit next to him at his business meeting at the airport? Drive them back and forth to school and violin lessons?

"The next time he threatens you with taking full custody of the children," I told Andrea, "look him straight in the eye and say, 'You don't need your attorney for that. They're yours. In fact, here's their schedule so you know what they have to do when.' Then hand him the calendar for the next month."

"But, Dr. Leman," she said, "what if he takes me up on it?"

"He might," I said, "but then you need to use that time wisely. Go back to school. Cram in classes and finish your degree. If you're going to be a single mom, you need all the job skills you can get in order to provide for yourself and your children." I smiled. "But I can guarantee you that even if he does take the kids, it likely won't last a month."

I was right. It didn't even last a week. She nipped his controlling in the bud by standing up to him.

If you had to do it all over again, it's doubtful you'd pick the same man. But since you did pick that man, your attitude about the consequences will make all the difference in the future for you and your children. But there's also a line you have to draw and never step over.

The rest of this section may not be for all of you, but for others of you it'll be a lifesaver. Some of you picked up this book as a last-ditch effort. You've tried everything to change your husband. You feel so hurt, dissed, abused, and totally disregarded by your husband that you don't even know where to start thinking about the possibility of having a new husband by Friday. Yours has been unfaithful, has been physically or verbally abusive (or both), has denigrated you at every turn, and has even harmed your children, and you can't take it anymore. You want a new husband by Friday, that's for sure, but you're not certain if you want the *same* husband. You'd rather start all over. You no longer feel any love for this man you married because he has harmed you so much.

If so, what I'm going to say next is especially for you.

ARE YOU TRYING TO TURN YOUR ZEBRA INTO A HORSE?

Most guys *want* to please their wives—at least the healthy guys do. The guys who are good, moral men know what's right and act on it (even if they are dumb about relationships sometimes). But you might not have married a healthy guy.

Maybe your husband spends his time smoking weed, smashed on vodka, or loving the white lady of cocaine. Maybe he's a philanderer (openly or secretly) or a wife beater. Maybe he lives in the zone of pornography, and you're sickened just by the sight of him and what he forces you to do. Then let me ask you: Was he *ever* the husband you could respect, love, and prize? Or are you trying to take a zebra and turn him into a white stallion?

Here's what I mean. Some people who hear hoofbeats would say, "Oh, here comes a zebra." But if you live in the state of Illinois, chances are good that it's a horse coming, not a zebra. Yet people tend to believe what they want to believe. Is that you? Did you fall into the trap of trying to paint your husband-to-be as something other than he was? Then I have news for you. You can't rub the stripes off that zebra and make it a horse. It is what it is.

> *You can't rub the stripes off that zebra and make it a horse. It is what it is.*

A lot of single or single-again women go looking for the man of their dreams—their knight in shining armor, the gentle, loving, relational man who will want to stick around for a lifetime—in singles' bars. You might as well look for a zebra strolling down Lakeshore Avenue or riding up the escalators at Water Tower Place in Chicago.

Just watching the crude behavior of these types of men and listening to the language they use when talking about their ex-wives or ex-girlfriends will give you a clear picture of who these men are. Most don't like themselves very much, so how could they like—or love—anyone else? They go from job to job and relationship to relationship, finding fault with everyone but themselves.

> *Can this type of man change? It's possible. But it would take a lightning hit from the Almighty.*

Many have tempers. Most are looking for someone to do the mattress mambo with for a night or two; they're not looking for a long-term relationship.

I ask you, is the environment of a bar what you want for your home? For you? For your children? Is a man who will hang out in bars really the kind of man you want as your lifelong partner?

Can this type of man change? It's possible. But it would take a lightning hit from the Almighty. Some men are just losers. They're not capable of being the kind of strong men who are able to love a woman and treat her the way she deserves. Perhaps it's due to their background—the way they were treated at home (or the lack of a home) as they were growing up. Maybe it's due to their chemical dependency. But some men are downright incapable of thinking of anyone but themselves.

If this is the case for you, I'm sorry. I'm sorry you married a man who isn't capable of being a good lover or of thinking of anyone other than himself. You know now that you made a lousy choice; back then you were blinded by what you thought was love but what became rigid control and possessiveness.

If it comforts you, you are not alone. The world is full of such men. In my counseling practice, I've met some guys who are—to put it mildly—creeps. They'd bed anything that moved, and they just about do. They break their vows of marital faithfulness over and over again.

One man told me, in front of his wife, "I'm a good husband. I've only had four or five other women since I've been married. I don't know why that's not good enough for her."

You know what my advice was to that woman, after several counseling sessions of hearing the same kind of nonsense from her husband? "Dump the chump!" Without intervention from almighty God, that man was simply incapable of love, and that woman and her children had suffered under him for 23 years. Now her children were out of the home, and that woman needed and deserved to be free of his abuse. She had paid for her crime of falling in love with him for long enough.

If you look backward in your relationship, do you see early signs that your husband was a controller? Did you make excuses for him? The profile for a controller is that he's always right. When he's wrong, it's someone else's fault, never his. So he always needs a scapegoat. And his psychological (or physical) punching bag is . . . guess who? You.

It has to stop. Now.

Maybe when you married him, you thought you could change him. You've spent your entire marriage trying to accomplish that, and it's not working. He may have a decent job, but morally he's bankrupt. Behaviorally he's bankrupt because he didn't grow up in a healthy environment. He's patterning the dishonesty, arrogance, laziness, infidelity, and abuse he saw in his own home. If you started out with a man who came from a dysfunctional background, the chances of your husband doing a 180 are slim, even if you follow every principle in this book.

Can such a man change? Sure, there's always hope. But spiritual renewal is about the only way I know of to change that guy. You can try to rub the stripes off that zebra until your hands are raw, but he'll still be a zebra, not a horse.

If you don't start with good, quality material in building your house, the foundation will crack, then the walls, and eventually the entire house will cave in. The foundation of your marriage has to be built right—cemented with the mortar of trust, mutual admiration, mutual respect, and kindness. Without that, you need to be realistic: your marriage isn't going to last. Or if it does, at what price? What price will you and your children (if any) pay by allowing your husband to continue treating you as he is?

Some women live every day with a husband who drinks, carouses, parties, and picks up and sleeps with other women. Is that really what you want the rest of your life to be like? Your husband needs professional help. If he's not willing to get that help, then you need to make some choices for you and your future, especially if children are involved.

Ask Dr. Leman

Q: I've been married for 25 years. Our marriage should be good. I'm the firstborn, and Hal's the baby of the family (I just read your book *Born to Win*)—but he was one of those manipulative, scheming babies who got away with everything. He took advantage of his own mother in just about every situation imaginable.

During our marriage, Hal's had three affairs—one just a month after we got married, one ten years into our marriage, and one just last year. He even took one of my girlfriends out to make me jealous!

I've had it. But I grew up in a home where divorce wasn't an option, and I can't get that out of my head. I told him we needed to talk, and he said, "What about?" I told him I needed a break—from him. He agreed not to tell our teenage daughter anything but good-bye. But he came back later, when he knew I'd be gone for an hour, and told her that he didn't want to leave but I was making him leave. He never told her about his affairs. He just said everything was my fault. I don't want to bad-mouth the father of my child, but what do I do? Help! I'm drowning.

Elise, Rhode Island

A: You're the classic pleaser married to the controller. Controllers are usually firstborns, but you can find a sociopathic type of personality at the bottom of the family as well. That's what you have. All these years he's been bleeding you dry and taking advantage of you. It needs to stop. He's had it good all these years—he can come and go from home as he pleases, his laundry gets done, he's fed, he's not accountable to anyone, and he's having sex with other women on the side (and probably still with you). Why would he want to leave home or change?

But in this case, you need to take a stand. That man can no longer be welcome in your home. Your daughter, as a teenager who has watched how her daddy has treated you, needs to be told the truth (not the blow-by-blow version, mind you, but the overall detail that her father has had three affairs during your marriage). Meet with an attorney to see what your options are. Now is your time to play hardball. Do you really want to live the rest of your life like this? You—and your daughter—are worth more than that.

Checkup, Anyone?

Every six months I go to the dentist. You know, the dentist sends you the card that says, "Kevin, it's that time again. Time to clean the ivories."

The last time I was in for a checkup, I teased my dental hygienist, "You get awfully happy over the fact that I floss."

"Now, Dr. Leman," she said, "you know how important that is."

Yes, I know, so I buy the stupid plastic things at Walgreens to make flossing easier. I'm not a great flosser, but I'm better than I used to be. We all need those checkups once in a while. If we don't take care of the plaque, it could build up on our teeth and lead to dental problems. If we don't have doctor checkups, cholesterol could build up in our veins and cause a major heart attack.

In the same way, your marriage needs a checkup once in a while. If you're married to a user, you have to stand up for yourself. You have to develop "no" power. You owe it to yourself, your kids, and the next generation.

I once received a poignant letter from a woman who was in deep shock. Through her husband's carelessness, she found a receipt for some flowers he'd purchased midday at a local grocery store. They were described as "Special $12.99 Roses." So, of course, she was expecting roses to show up. Then she looked at the date on the receipt. It was three days earlier on a weekday.

She began to be suspicious that her husband was having an affair. What did this smart woman do? She hired a private investigator to tail the sucker and got the whole report about where he'd been and what he'd done, including pictures.

Turns out that her husband, who was in sales, had been shacking up with her best friend (whom she'd known since high school) during lunch a couple of blocks away from her house. The other woman's husband was an airline pilot and gone for three or four days at a time. These were women who went out to lunch together, whose kids were in soccer together, who talked eyeball to eyeball about haircuts, fashions, shoes, and kids.

"Dr. Leman," she asked, "what do I do?"

"You go to your girlfriend," I said, "and you say, 'So, are you going to tell your husband, or am I?' You talk straight with your husband too, and show him the proof. Then you watch the proverbial stuff hit the fan."

Sure, you could try counseling if you're in that situation, but usually the hurt is so deep and devastating, and the violation of the marriage and a friendship so profound, that there would be little chance of your relationship being put back together. The hurt simply doesn't go away; the reminders are too many and too personal.

As you might have guessed, this couple didn't make it. The husband couldn't understand why it was such a big deal to his wife ("It was just sex; it wasn't like a relationship," he told her), and the wife refused to put up with such thinking or behavior (and rightfully so). Within a month, she began to pursue a divorce. She confronted both her husband and her best friend separately and told them directly how much they had hurt her, violated her trust, and done irreparable damage to both families.

Because she couldn't rid her mind of the images of the two of them together and still live in the neighborhood, she found a home in a town nearby (20 minutes away). She kept her same job but moved the children to a smaller school so neither she nor they would be in contact with her former best friend or her children any longer. She pursued a sharp attorney who protected her rights and her children's rights while allowing them to have weekend and holiday contact with their father.

She told me in a follow-up session that when the shocking news circulated around their rather close neighborhood, her former best friend had left for work one day . . . and didn't come back. Her husband received an email saying that she thought it was best she move to another state, and that she was granting him full custody of the children. That man stepped up to the plate. He rearranged his work schedule so he could work from home four days a week. On Friday and often half of Saturday, his mother, who lived an hour away, took care of his two children (who were four and seven) so he could finish any projects that needed office time.

If you've faced a similar situation—you've been betrayed and your trust has been violated by people close to you—you aren't alone. It happens to women across the nation every day—and with their best friends. (Ironically, the woman I counseled and her husband were the two people voted "most likely to marry and live happily ever after" in their senior class in high school.)

So you call your attorneys, and you begin divorce proceedings. But the tough thing about divorce is that everyone pays. Kids pay emotionally; you pay financially, relationally, and emotionally; and your husband (although he might not seem sorry now) will pay down the road in his future relationships.

That's why it's worth it to:

1. Set time aside to really get to know your man. Observe how he interacts with his family. Watch how his dad treats his mom and how his mom treats his dad. These are all clues to how your husband was treated growing up and to discovering what patterns he will continue to follow in his relationship with you. (For some of you, this advice can help you choose more wisely the second time around.)
2. Make sure you put each other first and communicate every day to keep your heart connection close.
3. Don't go to bed angry.
4. Don't leave issues unresolved.

Ask Dr. Leman

Q: My husband lies about everything. He lied on his job application about smoking, drinking, and drug usage (I've caught him snorting cocaine seven times over the past couple years). He's always very secretive and doesn't like me going into the den when he's working late at night. He constantly maxes out our credit card, making major purchases (like a boat I've never been on!) without talking to me about it, and he's getting us deeply into financial trouble. What do I do?

A: Confront that man. Tell him immediately you need to talk. Tell him that he needs professional help for his chemical dependency. With his secretive behavior, it's also quite possible that he's hooked on pornography and he doesn't want you to know. To find out for sure, click on the "history" button on his computer, and you'll be able to track what he's viewed recently.

Has he asked you to perform sex acts that you would consider kinky or that you're uncomfortable with? Has he forced you to do things you don't want to do sexually? That's another clue he might be involved in pornography.

Also, check out the charges on your credit card to see what exactly they are. Again, you might find pornography is involved. If so, confront him. Don't say, "Are you watching pornography?" if you know it's true. Don't give him the wiggle room to get out of it. Instead, say, "I know you're involved with pornography. It's filthy, disgusting, and degrading to all women and to me, and it has to stop. I won't allow you to live in this home if you continue such practices. You need to make an appointment immediately with a counselor to talk about that and about your continual lying." If you are a cosigner, you may want to put a hold on that credit card and not allow any more charges.

That man is using you. Don't tolerate his behavior. You need to insist he get professional help; if not, he needs to leave your home and not be allowed back in. A liar can't be trusted, and neither can a sexual pervert. He has no place in your home.

"No" Power

If there is abuse of any kind (physical, sexual, emotional, or verbal) in the marital relationship, I draw the line. Your husband, preferably, has to leave, or you do. You cannot remain in the same household. If that means bringing things to a head, so be it. If your husband is physically abusive, though, make sure you have carefully laid out your plans about when you can pack and leave (when he's not home) and where you can go to be safe in both the short term and the long term.

"But, Dr. Leman," you say, "he's a deacon in the church. It'll embarrass him and ruin his ministry."

I don't care who he is. He could even be the pastor of the church. (Such abuse happens more often than we think.) You cannot put yourself or your children in harm's way because of an abusive male. You also can't live on eggshells 24-7, waiting for the next blowup.

You can try counseling first. You can say, "Listen, I'll go with you, I'll hold your hand, I'll be your cheerleader if you're willing to change, but I can't do it for you. You have to handle this one-on-one and face it."

You have to say no and put the responsibility back in his court. Let me say this clearly: You weren't put on this earth to be walked on by anyone, especially your husband. You do not have to be a slave dog to your guy. You are worth far more than that.

You can't live on eggshells 24-7, waiting for the next blowup.

If you give a controller an inch, he'll take a mile. That's why you have to draw the line firmly and quickly and have high standards. If your husband is cussing you out, swearing at you, and telling you you're no blanking good, you should not tolerate that. At all. Any kind of intimidating, disrespectful behavior isn't to be tolerated in marriage for *any* reason.

I've actually encouraged women to file papers for divorce just to get the man's attention—to show that she means business and is taking action. At times, believe it or not, that can bring an abusive man to the point of realizing he's been wrong and he needs counseling and help.

With a lot of hard work on both parts, sometimes those relationships can be saved. That's a big "sometimes," because the learning patterns are so ingrained that they're hard to shake.

There are times you have to take the buzzard by the beak. You have to say, "This is not going to work. And I refuse to cover for you or allow this behavior anymore." You don't stay to argue. You say it once, turn your back, and walk away.

Women Talk

My husband's been an alcoholic for 17 years. I used to call and cover for him at work when he got drunk. Then I heard you speak at a seminar about not being the enabler. I went home that day and decided to give it a try. My husband drank so much that night that he was hung over the next day. Usually I call in to work and tell them he's not feeling well and will be a little late. My husband gets away with it since his boss doesn't come in until 11. But that next morning I didn't call in. I just let the phone ring when his work called to see where he was.

Hal was furious with me when he woke up. "Why didn't you answer the phone?" he yelled. I told him I wouldn't cover for him anymore. I wouldn't lie for him anymore. I was done.

When he got into work that day, he'd missed a really important meeting and his boss noticed. Let's just say the boss wasn't happy, and Hal ended up having to work most of that night. When he missed another morning at work, his boss caught on to him. He told him that if he wanted to keep his job, he'd have to go to AA. So now Hal goes. He's not always happy about it, but he goes. He still drinks way more than I'm comfortable with, but he's stopped yelling at me. You're right, Dr. Leman. It is all about consequences, and it worked. Our home is calmer now than it's been for years.

Janet, Texas

Where do I draw the line? There are two actions that are completely unacceptable.

Physical or sexual abuse and threats that he'll hurt or kill you or your children. You should *never* stay in a marriage where your husband physically abuses you, sexually abuses you, or threatens your life and physical well-being with a gun or a knife. For your sake and for the sake of your children (if any), you need to move quickly to make a plan to get out. But you also have to be smart. You need to move out at an opportune time when doing so won't put you or your children in danger. In other words, assuming your husband has a job and goes to a work site or an office, you need a well-thought-out escape plan.

Contact the local women's shelter in advance to get specifics and suggestions about how to handle the next steps for your own and your children's well-being. Although a women's shelter is temporary and you need to have a long-term plan in mind for where you can go, the staff there are trained to assist you with the initial time of crisis.

You need to form a plan for where you're going and what you need to do to get out the door and stay out. Perhaps after your husband goes to work, you pack necessities for you and the children, pick the children up from school, and go directly to the women's shelter. The staff there is trained to handle angry men, and you need that kind of protection. Going to your girlfriend's several blocks away is not a good plan, especially if your man angers easily and is violent. He might go to your girlfriend's and take you out, take your girlfriend out, and take your children out. Many wives in this country are murdered by their husbands—even if they have restraining orders against them. You need to get out, get away, seek legal counsel, and file charges with the authorities.

Love never demands its own way. If it does, it's not love, and you cannot be fooled and hope for the best.

Emotional and verbal abuse. "But, Dr. Leman, he's not kicking me around," you say. "He just yells at me and tells me I'm no good."

Emotional and verbal abuse is just as damaging, though, as physical abuse. Words hurt; they last. And if your children are seeing this and are the subject of the same kind of abuse, the same results apply. You cannot continue to stay in an abusive relationship.

In physically, sexually, emotionally, and verbally abusive situations, you have to take control and get yourself and your children (if any are involved) away from that male controller. If you are a pleaser who wants the oceans of life to be smooth and will do anything to avoid a confrontation, this will be extremely difficult. Like a moth to a flame, you were drawn to this guy because he was so in control of everything. But you have to get out. This is not only an unhealthy situation, it's a dangerous one.

> *You need to take control of your life. If you can't do it for yourself, do it for your children.*

You need to take control of your life. If you can't do it for yourself, do it for your children. They're making notes every day on how your husband treats you. Let them see a mom who respects herself enough not to take abusive, disrespectful behavior.

No family is perfect, but children learn from their experiences at home that it is either a place where abuse and fear are allowed to reign, or a place where love and respect are the cornerstones of a satisfying relationship. Which experience do you want to pass on to the next generation?

I applaud you for your courage in doing what you need to do.

Wednesday

Think about What You Want to Say, Then Divide It by Ten

How to talk so your guy will really listen . . . and listen so your guy will really talk.

I hate to fly coach. Yes, you can think I'm a snob, and I'll admit to being partly snobbish about this fetish. But the real reason I need to be in the front part of the airplane is that I get terribly claustrophobic (this from a man who flies several times a week). Maybe I should see a psychiatrist. Maybe he could help me!

Anyway, the prime seat for me on the airplane is always the very first seat on the right-hand side. It's the one place where no one in front of me can put the seat back, which helps my claustrophobia greatly. But once in a while, despite my best, charming efforts, I find myself stuck in coach.

The bad news is that I'm in coach. The really bad news is that there's only one seat in coach I can survive in. In an MD-80, that seat is 7D, because it juts out a little bit into the aisle, and I don't have that closed-in feeling. Well, I got stuck in 7D once when Sande was with me, and she dutifully sat in 7E, the middle seat. There was another woman sitting in 7F, the window seat.

It wasn't long after we were settled in for a flight from Tucson to Chicago—that's 3 hours, 20 minutes—that Sande struck up a conversation with the woman next to her. They talked for the better part of two and a half hours—nonstop. I could have given my wife a 100-question quiz on this Jane Doe's life, and Sande would have passed with flying colors.

I was amazed at what they talked about—children, grandchildren, cooking, girlfriends, their relationships with their sons-in-law, Tucson, Chicago, the daughter who went to school in Chicago. They even swapped some recipes they could remember off the top of their heads. Point is, they talked and they talked. Every once in a while I would come up for air from my headphones, and they would still be talking.

So Sande meets a complete stranger and talks straight for two and a half hours of a 3-hour, 20-minute flight. They got to know each other well in a short period of time. Then there's me with my headphones on. I've flown nearly four million miles on American Airlines alone, but there are many flights when I get on, see a fellow in the window seat, and say, "Good morning." That's it. Two words. On a trip from Tucson to Chicago, that's an average of one word every hour and 45 minutes.

> *Every once in a while I would come up for air from my headphones, and they would still be talking.*

You see, I have no need to get to know the guy next to me. I just don't. But Sande, and women like her, really enjoy that "sharing" communication. Once again, it's what makes men and women so marvelously different from each other. Women lined up in a restroom at a concert or athletic event strike up a discussion. Men just want to go in, do their job, and get out.

I don't have stretch marks. I've never had a period. But my wife tells me I have a nose like a beagle for relationships. I can smell a rat (make that "a loser guy") at twelve feet. I've spent years living with women (a wife and four daughters), counseling women, and observing women.

Recently, when I was in a mall, I saw the enthusiastic meeting of three friends at the mall. The conversation went something like this.

"Oh, Molly, I love your hair! It's *adorable*," woman #1 said, after hugs had been exchanged.

And that was the cue for Molly to go into a long dissertation. "Oh my goodness, I don't know. Don't mention it. With my angular chin, long neck, and nose, I wanted it layered and feathered like this"—she took out a picture of what she was supposed to look like—"but the hairstylist did it all wrong. I have to go with Richard to his company party next week, and I just don't know how to fix it."

"Oh, it's not that bad," woman #1 said.

"And your shoes and your outfit . . . they're so *unusual*. Wherever did you get them?" woman #2 added.

Molly shrugged. "Oh, I just wanted to try something new. You really like them?"

"You can make anything look good," woman #1 said.

After another five minutes of constant chatter (I was sitting there drinking a Starbucks and watching them, because I couldn't help myself), Molly took her leave.

And you know what those other two friends said?

"Oh my, that haircut. How embarrassing. But I could never tell her. It'd hurt her feelings," woman #1 said.

"And that *outfit*," woman #2 added. "She looked like my 5-year-old in dress-up mode. With really big hips. That did not do her any favors. You know, I was thinking about getting *my* hair cut differently. . . ."

And off they went to continue their discussion.

Compare that with two husbands meeting at the mall.

"Ken." A handshake.

A nod. "Kevin."

"Nice weather we're havin."

"Yup."

Then, if we're feeling really social, one of us will add a comment.

"Got a haircut, huh?"

"Yup."

That's it. The extent of the conversation. And you know what? We're satisfied.

I can guarantee you those men didn't notice each other's outfits, or, if the clothes registered faintly, that image was forgotten the instant he walked off.

Women Talk

We've made significant progress in our marriage since we started applying the principles you talked about at our church seminar last month. My biggest struggle in marriage has been that my husband doesn't communicate the way I feel he ought to. The lightbulb went on when you said, "He's not your girl-friend, he's your husband." Sounded simple, but applying that truth has been life changing. And it took me only 17 years of marriage to figure that out (with your help). Guess I'm a slow learner, huh?

Alicia, Texas

But notice the biggest difference about these interactions: the word count used. Did you know that you use seven times the amount of words that your husband does every day—even on the days when you don't feel like talking to others?

I took an impromptu poll of women recently. I talked to ten married women and asked them what bugs them the most about their guy. Nine out of ten said, "He doesn't talk to me," and they followed it with, "I can't get him to do anything." Think about it this way: if you're always talking, then why does he need to?

You see, your guy is pragmatic. Enough words are flying in the air; he doesn't feel led to add to them. And again, when you think he's not thinking, the computer between his ears is actually quite busy in its processing mode. He just needs time to think through the angles sometimes before he responds. If you're too pushy and anxious, he'll pick up on that pressure to perform, and he'll shut down *and* shut up.

After 40-plus years of marriage, I finally worked up enough courage to look my wife in the eye and tell her, "You're bossy."

> **Communication 101**
>
> 1. Realize he won't use as many words as you do.
> 2. Don't set up expectations that are unrealistic for the male species.
> 3. Be specific when something's bothering you.
> 4. Give the CliffsNotes, not the whole enchilada.
> 5. Don't expect a quick response; give him time to think.

Her response? "I'm not bossy. My ideas are just better than yours."

Now what could I say to that? Most of the time, she's right!

Good Communication Rules

If you want to have a new husband by Friday, here are a few simple rules.

Say It, but Divide It by Ten

If you take away anything from this chapter, let it be this one principle: the pathway to your husband's heart and mind is equidistant. If you get to his mind, you'll get to his heart. If you get to his heart, you'll get to his mind. But an excess flow of words will shut down your guy's attention every time. He won't say it, but he'll be thinking, *Could you just get to the point?* Your husband doesn't use as many words as you do, so don't assume he wants all the details like your girlfriend would. He doesn't. He wants the CliffsNotes so he can get the gist of the situation, then get on to solving the problem without wasting time.

So if you expect him to want the whole enchilada, you'll frustrate yourself and him. Men tend to be linear and lockstep in their thinking: this happened, then that happened, then that happened . . . 1, 2, 3. Women tend to go about their conversations in more of a circular fashion, telling what they feel first, then throwing in bits here or there about what actually happened. Along the way, they lose the linear male, who is trying to sort out what exactly happened and what you're so upset about. Women can follow the bouncing ball when it comes to conversation; men can't.

> *He won't say it, but he'll be thinking,* **Could you just get to the point?**

Your job isn't to spell out everything for your husband; it's to present the situation in as few words as possible. Then give him the courtesy of figuring it out on his own so he can help solve the puzzle. Men love to solve things, to crack the code. Doing so makes them feel like James Bond himself. So give the problem to him in short little sound bites, and let him run with it a bit. Even better, when he comes up with part of the solution, put your arm around him and say, "I'm so lucky to be married to you. You're so smart."

So give the info in *USA Today* style—compactly and only what he needs to know. *Give me the problem*, your husband is thinking, *and while you're talking, I'll get busy solving it*.

If you ask a question and get silence as your answer, either he's vegged out in front of the Super Bowl game, or you're being critical and he's learned to be careful about what he says. He won't come out and give his opinion until it's fully formed based on fact and research, and he knows exactly what he's going to say and how he's going to say it.

Don't Expect Him to Read Your Mind

"Sometimes I'm so tired of telling him what I want and need. Why can't he just know?"

Stop right there. He doesn't know. He doesn't have female body parts or female thinking. It's a no-win situation for him to try to guess what you're thinking, because he'll be wrong. Or maybe you tell him what your need is and that he needs to meet it, but even when he does, you say, "Well, that's my need all right, but you only met it because I told you to or asked you to. You don't really care about me." See what I mean? Your non-risk-taker husband isn't dumb enough to fall for that. He's your husband, not a mind reader.

So if you want your husband to know something, say something, or do something, simply ask him. No games. Be specific and straightforward, and communicate respectfully.

If you'd like to go away for a weekend, hints will never work. Just come right out and say it: "Let me tell you about what I'd love to have happen sometime. . . ."

> *If you want your husband to know something, say something, or do something, simply ask him. No games. Be specific and straightforward, and communicate respectfully.*

Touch him, look into his eyes, and then slip him the commercial announcement of what you'd like him to do.

Don't Ask Unnecessary Questions

If you already know the answer, don't ask the question.

"Did you mean to put the garbage out early?"

Well, duh, if the garbage can is outside, he evidently put it out early.

Are you ever going to hear this kind of explanation from your guy? "Of course I put it out early, because I read the paper and they're picking up early because of the holidays. You don't think I'm smart enough to figure out when to put the garbage out when I do this 52 weeks a year? And now you're questioning me? Boy, you sure don't respect me."

Tell, Don't Share

If you want to tell your husband something, then *tell* him, don't "share."

Tell him, "The dog drank out of the toilet bowl again and wet the rug. Any ideas how to stop that?" instead of, "I'm so mad. I can't believe it. That dog . . . ooh, he wet all over the rug *again*. It's the third time this week. And he's been drinking out of the toilet bowl again. I just knew we shouldn't have bought that dog. . . ." And the litany goes on.

Give your husband the CliffsNotes, then ask for his help. "The school called me today because Timothy got caught cheating on an exam," you say. "Here's what I need from you. I need to know what you think *I* ought to do, what you think *you* ought to do, and what you think *we* ought to do. Would you let me know?" State the problem and what you need your husband to do, then walk away and let him think through the situation.

Think of it this way. A woman's natural inclination is to share, to tell the whole story in every fine detail. You'll lose your husband's interest if you do so. You see, when you begin to talk, his knee-jerk reaction is, "Let me fix that." But you don't always want things to be fixed. You want him to listen, right? Realize that telling a man something without asking him to fix it is like putting a steak bone in front of a hungry dog and asking him not to salivate. But if you tell him up front what you want him to do, he'll curb those very natural urges (most of the time).

Say It Once, Then Skip the Nagging

If you want your husband to do something, try this wonderful three-step process, guaranteed to get results.

1. Say it once.
2. Turn your back and walk away.
3. Resist the temptation to remind him.

Here's what I mean. Let's say that at 6:00 on Saturday your friends, the Johnsons, are coming for dinner. The yard is a real mess from your husband's projects, and you'd like to get it picked up before your guests arrive. You're hoping he'll think of it himself, but he doesn't. So, at 10 in the morning on Saturday, you tell your husband, "Honey, the Johnsons are coming for dinner. Would you mind picking up the yard before they get here? Having our home look nice is important to me."

The typical male will nod in response. If he hasn't used his word count for the day yet, he might even say, "Okay, I'll do that."

So you go about your business to get other things done that day. But

Talking Male Code

When he says . . .
"Fine," it means he's angry.

"Whatever," it can mean (based on body language and tone): "It doesn't really matter to me, so whatever you want to do is fine," or, "I know you'll get your way anyway, so why fight it? Just do what you want."

"Not now," it means, "I don't want to deal with this right now. I don't want to tell you. I'm processing. Leave it alone."

"Okay, if that's the way you want it," it means, "I'll get even with you later. You haven't listened to me at all. I'm sick and tired of trying to make my point, so do whatever you want." (Then watch out—he's going to start playing the "Dump Truck, Dump Truck, Who's Got the Dump Truck?" game. You don't want to go there. It's a vicious cycle: if you have the right to dump on him, he has the right to dump on you.)

you don't see any action from your husband and you get antsy. You're afraid that he's forgotten. He's been puttering around in the garage, but there's no action on your front lawn. So, if you're anything like Mrs. Uppington (my beloved wife), half an hour later you remind him. "Uh, honey, are you still going to pick up the yard?"

"Yup," he says, and continues on his project.

Give it a couple more hours, and you're starting to steam. After all, it's 2:00, and the Johnsons are coming in four hours. You're really going to be embarrassed if the yard is such a mess. If you remind him again, get prepared for a sullen husband who isn't going to be helpful now—or ever again.

What you haven't taken into account is the male mind-set. Here's what he's thinking: *She told me at 10 in the morning to pick up the yard. Okay, I'll do that. I want to finish my project in the garage first. Let's see, they're coming at 6, and it takes me 10 minutes to take a shower and clean up, so if I attack the yard at 4, I'll have plenty of time.* And off he goes with his plan for the day.

> *Each of us has our own private logic—the way we look at life.*

Your husband has every intention of doing what you ask. Remember, he wants to please you. He's even scheduled what you want done in his day. But reminding him short-circuits his "want to" and his pleasure in doing something for you. Every time you remind him, he's thinking, *What, you don't think I can keep anything in my head for a few hours? Of course I'm going to get that done.*

Each of us has our own private logic—the way we look at life. If you tell your husband the two of you need to be somewhere at a specific time, most men will calculate in their mind, *Okay, let's see here. We have to be there by 7. The traffic that time of day is pretty slow—after rush hour. So we'll need to leave by 6:10.* He also figures out the best way to get from point A to point B and has it all plotted out.

Now, will your man say this to you? "By the way, honey, I know we have to be there at 7, and in an effort to please you, I was listening to the news to get the report on the traffic. I've figured out that we'll have plenty of time if we leave at 6:10 and take the expressway to the Ohio exit. We'll even get there early."

Can you *imagine* your husband saying that to you? Nuh-uh. Ain't gonna happen. But it doesn't mean he hasn't figured it all out in his head already.

If you nag him and remind him, he's psychologically rolling his eyes and telling himself, *She just doesn't understand me, does she? I know that stuff. I don't have to be told again.*

Take, for instance, my dear wife, Sande, a true firstborn if ever there was one. We were on our way to the Social Security office (I've reached the age where I need to consider such things), and she had told me three times that we needed to leave soon. Not one time, not two times, but three times. I don't need to be told that. I know exactly how long it will take me to get to the Social Security office—25 minutes. And mark my words, it'll be 25 minutes.

We're two completely different creatures, but we can still learn to get along fabulously. How you use your words makes all the difference.

If you want to make your husband feel like an idiot, continue to remind him of what he's supposed to be doing and when. Just keep talking. Nagging always creates a resentful husband.

Don't go there. Give your husband some credit for being a grown-up, and he'll act like one (well, at least most of the time—there's still that little boy in all of us). Tell him once, and then let the information go into his computer to be swirled around until he solves the problem.

"But, Dr. Leman," you're saying, "if I did that, I'd never get anything done around the house. He simply wouldn't do it."

Really? Are you so sure? Why not try an experiment in the next couple days to see if you get a happier, more helpful husband by Friday?

1. Say it once.
2. Turn your back and walk away.
3. Resist the temptation to remind him.

And if he doesn't get it done, then add another step:

4. Let reality be the teacher.

These steps work for children (I used them in my book *Have a New Kid by Friday*), and they work for the children's father too. If he doesn't get his project done, then let reality be the teacher.

Let's say you ask your husband to deposit his paycheck in the bank on the way home from work, to make sure it covers the large check you have to send to Visa the next day. He forgets, and you find the paycheck in his pants pocket four days later. That same day you get a letter from the bank, saying your Visa check has bounced and outlining the fees you need to pay—plus your bank account is overdrawn.

Do you take care of this yourself? Do you call up the bank or run over there immediately to apologize and take care of it? Do you call Visa and promise to get a new check to them right away? Do you then go to your husband, wag your finger, and say, "This is all your fault. I told you to deposit that check, and now look what's happened!"

No, you simply place his paycheck and the letter from the bank on his dinner plate (or somewhere else you know he'll find it). If he asks you to take care of the problem, your answer needs to be no. You already asked him to take care of it once and he didn't, and now he needs to deal with the consequences and follow up himself. The next time you ask him to do something, I bet he'll file that request as a priority, don't you?

You don't need to play judge. Just let reality be the teacher.

So say it once. Be specific. Give your husband a day that a task needs to be done, a time it needs to be done (if any specific deadline), and the reason it needs to be done. "Honey, the Johnsons are coming tonight at 6. I'd like to have the yard picked up and done before they come, since you said you wanted to barbecue ribs on the grill. I know you'd like the lawn to look as nice as I would."

Ordering your husband to do a task will only cause him to dig his crab claws into the earth and not move forward. He'll revert to his "no one's going to tell me what to do" basic male response to orders. No male likes to be ordered around, especially by a woman. I know that may sound terribly sexist, but it's true.

One wife told me her husband got grumpy every time she asked him to do anything, even getting something down for her from a cupboard above her head. Finally she asked him, "Why don't you want to help me?"

"I don't like it when you order me around."

She was stunned. "When I ask you to please get something from the cupboard to help me, that's ordering you around?"

"It sure feels like it. It's all in your tone."

"So how am I supposed to ask for help then?" she asked.

He shrugged. "Just make me a list. I'll take it from there."

So there you have it—there's a reason for those "honey-do" lists (if they're not overwhelmingly long). They give a man something to refer to and don't have a "tone."

> **Husbands Can Say the Stupidest Things**
>
> When your husband says something stupid, don't say, "How could you even *think* of such a thing?" Don't give the disgusted, you're-out-to-lunch look. Instead, look him straight in the eye and say, "Tell me more about that."
>
> The key is to keep your man talking so you know what he's up to (but that's your secret!).

Remember Grandma's wise words: "You catch more flies with sugar than with vinegar." She was right.

Keep in mind that your husband has a need to perform. He wants to know he measures up in your eyes. So you could say, "I know you're busy and up to your eyeballs with work, even on a Saturday, but we're having company over tonight. I know I'm asking a lot and don't know if you could squeeze it in, but I'd really love to have the yard cleaned up so everything looks nice when we have those barbecued ribs you wanted to make. If you're too busy, I can try to find someone else to do it. Just let me know."

That puts the ball firmly in your husband's court. Most guys would rather do the labor themselves than pay someone to edge their lawn and clean up the dog doo.

How you approach your husband with your words makes all the difference. But he needs it to be his idea, and he doesn't have to be reminded once you've asked him. The trust factor is huge in this. You need to trust that he's going to follow through on what you asked him to do, without reminding him like you do your child. He's not your 6-year-old; he's your husband.

> **9 Things You Can Say to Get Your Man's Attention**
>
> "Honey, help me understand something."
> "I don't have a clue, and I really need your help."
> "Can I tap into that wonderful, logical, linear-thinking brain of yours?"
> "You're so good at . . . [*fill in the blank*]."
> "I wish I could think like you."
> "I was wondering. Do you think it would be a good idea to . . . [*fill in the blank*]"?
> "I'm sorry. Would you forgive me?"
> "I can't get enough of you."
> "What do you think?"

Learn to Respond, Not React

When you respond, you assess the situation, decide what you're going to do, and then act as a result. When you react, you let your emotions take over your head. In far too many marriages, the spouses react to each other rather than taking the time to respond.

Let's say you asked your husband to fix the dishwasher. You tell him that you really need it fixed by Sunday, because the next week is going to be crazy and you need all the help you can get—including not having to hand wash the dishes. Sunday comes and goes. By Wednesday you've had it. Do you call him up at work and rail on him: "You *promised* to fix that dishwasher!" Do you give him the silent treatment at dinner? No, you call a repairman.

> *Every guy likes to solve his own problems before he gets "help" from another guy.*

Your husband might be dumb as mud, but he will have a clue that something's working when he sees you putting dishes in the dishwasher again. He'll ask, very logically, "Hey, is the dishwasher working again?"

"Sure is," you can respond. "I got it fixed today."

He'll look puzzled. "Fixed?"

"Yeah. I needed it fixed, so I called the repairman. He came right over. The bill's on the counter."

You say it (nicely), turn your back, and walk away. You don't harangue your husband with, "You should have done it yourself. It would have saved us $180, but no, you decided to be lazy." Instead you just state the facts and walk away. Problem solved.

Chances are, you'll leave him behind thinking, *Hmm, she asked me to fix it. But I didn't do it. And she's not mad. She just got it done.*

I bet you anything the next time you ask him to get something done, he'll get right on it. Every guy likes to solve his own problems before he gets "help" from another guy. He needs to know you'll give him a chance to do it and you won't pester him, but he also needs to know you won't wait forever for what you need.

A little reality therapy goes a long way toward getting a new husband by Friday.

Let's say your husband was supposed to pick up your daughter after school, in order for you to finish up your work and be ready by 7 to go to a dinner for his work. He forgets to pick up your daughter, and the school calls, so you have to go get her. At 6:30 your husband calls out, "Honey, are you just about ready?" (He ought to know better. After doing your work as a lab pharmacist and then getting caught in the rain as you picked up your daughter, you look like something the cat dragged in.)

You could get snippy and say, "Well, do I *look* like I'm ready?" or, "I'm not ready because I had to pick up *your daughter* since you forgot."

Or you could take a deep breath and say, "Honey, I still need to take a shower. It will take me 40 minutes to do what I need to do before we get out the door." And when he looks at you with surprise, tell it straight, but kindly. "When you didn't pick up Megan today, that put me 40 minutes behind schedule. We're just going to have to be late."

What a man doesn't want is to be late for a work event, so he'll get the idea.

If your husband criticizes you at dinner, then wants you to roll around in the hay with him that night, just say no. "I don't feel like having sex with you right now because you criticized me all through dinner. That doesn't make me feel romantic in the least."

You see, B doesn't happen until A is completed. You're not going to be a willing partner for sex until you and your husband talk through what happened at dinner.

So tell him what's bothering you, and be specific. He can't help solve something if he doesn't know it upset you.

Ask Dr. Leman

Q: I can't take it anymore. I'm sick of my husband blowing me off every time I ask for help. I tell him I need help, I ask for help, and nothing happens. It's like it doesn't even register. I get left holding the bag, doing all of his "stuff," because he doesn't get around to it. He doesn't talk, he doesn't help. He's a big nada in my life. I've had it. I need some quick help.

Andrea, Maryland

A: Every time your husband doesn't help you, what's going on in your mind? You're probably thinking things like, *He just doesn't care. He doesn't really love me. I don't even exist to him. Why did I marry this guy anyway?*

Frankly, you might have married a man from a very dysfunctional family. Maybe he's not capable of thinking past his own self. But more likely, he doesn't have a clue that his lack of help is sending a message to you that he doesn't give a rip about you.

Here's what I'd suggest. Have a sit-down with that man of yours. Don't hold back; tell it to him straight. "Today I asked for help with X. You didn't help. Every time you do that, it makes me feel like you don't care at all about what's important to me, and you don't care about me. If you really don't care, then I need to start making different plans. If you do, things need to change. This isn't working. I don't know if you're happy or not, but if it counts, I'm not happy. It might be working for you because I'm tucking the kids in at night, helping them with homework, doing your laundry, taking your mom to the doctor, and all those things. But it's not working for me. I feel disregarded and disrespected. And I don't want to live like this any longer."

Such a conversation is a tough one to have, because sometimes you'll like the results and sometimes you won't. If he really doesn't care whether he's in your life or not, wouldn't you rather know now than wait 20 years? And oftentimes this shock therapy can work wonders to wake up a man who is just living in his own zone, unaware of what you need. Either way, you need to know.

Soften the Blow

When you know you're going to offer a strong opinion and have reason to believe he may not see things the way you do, start by saying, "You know, I may not have a clue on this, but I think it would be a good idea if you talk to Roger again before we commit ourselves to doing the back addition on the house." (You're smart—you're admitting you may not have a clue. Your husband's defenses go down immediately.) "You know I'm not handy at things like that. But I think maybe we should run it by Roger again, just to make sure the cost is accurate. Again, I could be completely wrong." Saying this in a nonpushy way guarantees you'll get him to listen.

Pick Your Time to Talk

Choose your time wisely if you have something important to say to your husband. The last quarter of a football game isn't a good time to share with him. Right after one of you has paid the bills isn't a good time either, especially if you or your husband is thinking, *I don't know if we're going to make it this month.* If you ask at that point, you probably won't get the answer you want.

Keep Your "Honey-Do" List Short

Because you women are all such incredible multitaskers, you've always got more than one thing on your brain at a time. You feel the pressure of your job, children, and school, and just thinking about everything you have to get done makes you start another list that has to get done.

Let me encourage you to make your list for your husband short. One thing at a time is best—not because he's simpleminded, but because he's focused on getting one job done at a time. Then say, "There's one thing I'd like to get done in November." You're not saying he has to do it *now.* You're giving him the credit for believing he'll arrange his schedule to get this important thing done for you. Having some freedom to slot into his own schedule what you want done is very important to your husband.

Don't Talk about Him to Your Girlfriends

Never *ever* talk to your girlfriends about anything dumb your husband did. Don't share anything he's told you about stress he's under at work or about any personal situation. If you do, you are deeply violating his trust of you, his one and only. When a man dares to share, he's daring to share with you, not the whole world. Respect him enough to keep his confidences. You wouldn't like it if your secrets were blabbed to the world, would you? Then extend him the same courtesy.

> *Having some freedom to slot into his own schedule what you want done is very important to your husband.*

What you *can* do (and he'll welcome this kind of gossip) is tell your girlfriends what an incredible man you have, about something sweet or helpful he did, or about how thoughtful he is. Those are the kinds of things your girlfriends will tell their husbands (probably with a "How come *you're* not like that?" comment aimed their direction). When your girlfriends' husbands pass the good word back to your husband, his chest will puff out with contentment. *Wow, I'm such a lucky man. My wife really thinks I'm a great guy. What a woman I married!* That's the kind of gossip that does wonders for your man.

Even better, why not whisper those things in *his* ear? He'll be doing cartwheels for you in no time.

Say What You Mean; Don't Make Him Guess

I came home early recently to surprise Sande and take her out to dinner. "When do you want to go?" I asked.

"Oh, 6:00 sounds good."

"Where do you want to go?" I asked.

"Wherever you want to go," she said. "I want you to choose."

"Okay, let's go to the soup and salad place."

"Uh, honey, I don't like that place anymore."

"Well then, how about the Italian place?"

"No, I don't want to eat there. They put weird stuff on the food."

By now I was a little exasperated. "Then you pick!"

And on the conversation went. If Sande had told me up front that she had a hankering for salmon, that would have been all the information I'd need. I would have known exactly where to go, because she's had salmon at a certain restaurant before and raved about it.

One of my friends called me this week as Sande and I were getting ready to go somewhere. He wanted to come over for 15 minutes and talk.

"Sure," I said. "Come on over."

Sande poked her head into the room. "Leemie, wait a minute. He can't come over now. We have to get ready and leave by 5:00."

I checked my watch. That was an hour away from now. "Honey," I said, "it's Mark. He's a guy. When a man says he needs to talk for 15 minutes, he means 15 minutes."

She just lifted an eyebrow.

But it's true. A man says what he means. Contrast that to a woman, who says, "I'm just going to run in here for a few minutes. . . ." I ought to know. When my wife says that, I spend a lot

Talking At or Talking To?

Women in my counseling office have told me for years that they want to talk with their husbands. But when I dig a little deeper, what they mean is, "I want to talk *at* my husband." Women have no idea how much the steady flow of nonstop words can snow a man.

So let your guy be a guy—not a girlfriend.

of time parked on a bench outside the stores in the mall. (Good thing I can do a lot of my work by cell phone.) But you know why I do that? Because even if Sande is busy shopping, and that's not my natural inclination, I know that she enjoys my presence with her. That's worth spending some of my time, don't you think?

Don't Talk Down to Him

"Listen, Leemie, this is very important. I want you to get one lemon meringue pie and one pumpkin pie at Marie Callender's. Leemie, listen to me now, I want you to get this right. It's one lemon meringue pie and one pumpkin pie," Mrs. Uppington told me with her index finger raised. She was in full-blown firstborn mode. Like a teacher talking to a 6-year-old. But, you see, she'd already asked me the day before to get the pies and had given me the instructions about what kinds. I didn't need to get it again.

> **Heads Up**
>
> Telling him he's your man keeps him from becoming someone else's.

Your husband will sometimes act like the boy he once was, but he doesn't want to be treated like it.

Don't Pull Out the Tears

Women can be hormone driven. (Like I had to tell you that.) From the time they are pubescent at age ten, emotions run awry. Dr. Sande Leman, who has more than earned her doctorate in relationships as a mother of five and husband to said psychologist for 40-plus years, says that the worst possible age of all for women is ten years old. There's truth in that. Prepubescents are on the cutting age of adolescence. Their bodies are changing. Their hormones are changing. And PMS is well documented; it's not the "myth" that some misguided males still believe it to be (but then again, you knew that too).

I'm not saying men aren't emotional—they get emotional about fishing season, hunting season, football, and hockey, but that's a little different. Watch two pairs of children exit a school at the end of their day. What are two 10-year-old girls doing? Walking hand-in-hand, looking at each other, interacting, and sharing their feelings. What are two 10-year-old boys doing? Smacking each other upside the head, yelling, "Well, I can do X better than you. See?" Even young boys don't "share" feelings with each other; they act out their emotions.

Go back to what we talked about earlier. What's the #1 need for a woman in marriage? Affection. Was that on the man's list? No. His needs are to be respected, to be needed, and to be fulfilled. Your desire for affection covers a wide front. That's why if you don't get your daily dose of husbandly affirmation, things start going awry in your home.

But beware of too much emotion, since that shuts down a man. Tears make a husband feel helpless; he doesn't know what to do. In essence, you've neutered him. Tears aren't something he's wired to cope with. Yet a lot of women use tears to try to manipulate men.

It doesn't work. As soon as your husband sees tears, he has a terrible feeling inside him. *Uh-oh, did I cause that? Because if I did, I better get out of here quick.* Most men won't say, "Oh, honey, did I hurt your feelings? I'm so sorry!" They'll just drift away, thinking instead, *What the heck is wrong with her? I'm just going to watch TV until she gets over it.*

When you render a man helpless, you shut him down. Remember that he has a high need to please you (do you see that theme emerging in this book?), but he gets frustrated because he doesn't know how to do it. He's afraid if he tries, he won't measure up. For him, not being able to do something right is akin to someone telling you you're fat and ugly. You take it personally.

Your big, strong man who can pick up a big load, toss your kids up in the air and catch them, and pull away a tree limb that fell down is quite emotionally fragile. It goes back to the fact that he can count his good friends on only one hand—and most of the time, you're it. What you say matters.

Now, there are some men who simply don't get it. They are so oblivious to a woman's needs and emotions that they wouldn't see the big E at the ophthalmologist's office if it was a foot in front of them. I see a lot of those men. They're very perfectionistic non-huggers, like a tree that doesn't bend but stands erect. One friend of ours is like that. When Sande gives him an enthusiastic hug, he just stands there and doesn't move. These are the types of guys who are like robots, stiff and mechanical. If you follow them around, they're as boring as mud. They do the same things day after day. They mow their lawn the same way. They see life in terms of graph paper and stop signs, and in lockstep fashion. Everything about them is perfectionistic.

If you married a guy like this, what can you do? Well, you could knock on his forehead and say, "Knock, knock . . . is anybody in there?" If your husband was in my office, I'd tell him, "There's a party out there called life. If you need an invitation to join, here it is. Why not experience and enjoy life's ups and downs—and the highs and lows of living a life totally committed to another person? Why not risk an intimate connection?"

The problem with this type of guy, though, is that he would say, "I don't know why I'm here in counseling. I like life." That's because he's happy in the cocoon he's built around himself. That's who he is. And most likely, that was who he was when you married him.

So the question becomes: Why did you marry him? Were you so insecure that you needed the predictability of someone who would always do life the same way? That wears pretty thin after a few years, doesn't it?

You have a choice. Most women in this situation would dump the chump. After all, being the only person who tries to create any excitement in marriage can be frustrating and exhausting. And most robot-acting guys have tempers; they're strongly opinionated people who feel they know how everyone should act in life. They're not easy to change.

But I want you to think carefully through your decision first. *You* are the one who married this man. So are you going to make the best of your situation and go on to live life as fully as you can? No, you don't have the partner you wish you did. But you can make the best of what you do have by enjoying your family, your children, and your grandchildren.

Never Manipulate

Let's say you've been looking around your bedroom and thinking that things are looking a little shabby. You've been eyeing a new comforter and sheet set that costs $500. You know your tightwad husband will never go for that.

Then you notice he just bought new wheels for his truck. You don't really think he needed them, but then he didn't ask for your permission to buy them either. So you ask him, "How much did those wheels cost?"

Your husband flinches, taken off guard. "Uh, well, they were $165 apiece." He's thinking, *Now why's she asking me that?* He hasn't a clue. After all, he researched online and at four different shops to get the best price. With winter coming up, it was a smart choice.

Aha, you're thinking. *Sounds like a good time for me to get a new comforter and bedspread. After all, if he can spend $600 and some change on wheels, I could spend $500 on our bedroom.*

Now that's manipulation, and your husband won't appreciate it. Instead, why not try the best way? Be direct. Tell him in a few words what your needs and wants are.

"Honey, I noticed the other day that our bedspread is really faded and shabby. Having our bedroom look pretty is important to me. I checked a couple stores to see what the prices were and found a bedspread and sheets I liked for $500. Would it be okay with you if I bought them?"

Some of you are screaming at me now. "Dr. Leman, are you from the dinosaur age or something? Why would a woman have to ask her husband for *permission* to buy anything, especially when he went and bought something without her permission?"

> **Wise Advice**
>
> Date with your eyes wide open. Keep them half-closed after you're married.

Let me ask you something. Does your marriage mean something to you? Do you want to have a new husband by Friday? Then hear me out. Marriage is not about who wins the game. Marriage is about running the race together. If it takes two minutes for you to run the idea by your husband, isn't your marriage and having a happy hubby worth those two minutes? He probably didn't run the wheel purchase by you because he did all the research and the job was done, and what do you know (or care) about wheels and tires and car stuff anyway? He didn't do it intentionally to manipulate you. He just did it because that's what males do best—problem solve.

But if you manipulate your husband, you cross a line in marriage, and he has every right to feel angry. So don't go there. You're a smart woman—you figure it out. What do you have to lose? A happy, satisfied husband will do anything for you, including going to Bed, Bath & Beyond to help you lug that $500 comforter set back home. He might even help you set it up.

Accept His No as a No

Is there ever any possibility that when a man says no, a woman could let it go at that? Most women can't.

"Oh, honey, wouldn't it be fun to go see that today?" the wife says.

"No," the husband says.

Then the wife starts wheedling. "But I know you'd love it."

As her husband sits there, long in the jaws, he's thinking, *No way, no how, I'm not doing that. I'm not going, and that's final.*

If your husband says no, could you let it go at that? Without pushing for more information or asking why? Respect your husband enough to let his no be no.

If it's somewhere you want to go or something you want to do, why not say instead, "I respect your no as a no. But how about if I ran down there for a couple of hours?"

"Wait just one minute, Dr. Leman," some of you are saying. "Are you saying a woman has to ask her husband's *permission* to do something? Haven't you ever heard of women's lib?"

It's not that you need his permission to leave the house. Instead you're saying to your husband, "If you don't want to go there, do you mind if I do? Or do you have something else in mind for us here?" It's not *permission*; it's a respectful checking in.

Marriage is all about mutual respect.

Women Talk

I'm a very analytical person, and I know it. I used to always question what my husband said. But after hearing what you said, I realized I was telling my husband, "I don't think you can make decisions on your own for our family." I've made a conscious effort in the last six months to trust my husband's decisions for our family. In a strange way, I've felt relief. I feel closer to my husband, and he's been far more helpful than he used to be. He even got me roses last week, and it wasn't my birthday, Christmas, or Valentine's Day. It was just an ordinary day. Thanks for helping us get on the right track.

Nancy, Utah

Don't Just Go Through the Motions

The other day Sande and I were at Red Lobster, eating dead fish for a healthy lunch. Another couple entered the same time we did. They got their salads at the same time. When I was done eating, they were still eating. And you know what? Not a single word was exchanged between the two of them the entire time (ordering doesn't count). I mean *nothing*. Not even small talk.

Take a look around when you're in a restaurant, and you'll discover many couples just like them. They're not talking heart to heart, eyeball to eyeball. They're just going through the motions of being married.

Don't you want that intimate heart connection with your spouse? If so, your man needs to feel respected, needed, and fulfilled. He wants to know that when he says something, you will listen to him and honor his opinion as valid—even if you don't agree. If you do those things, you'll plant a deep desire within your husband to please you, respond to you, and listen to you when you want to talk.

Women Talk

*We've struggled for years in our marriage. Both of us have explosive tempers. Once when I asked Philip, "Why?" he said, "Well, it might just be a question to you, but it feels like an interrogation to me." The next day after our "discussion" (okay, let's just call it what it was—a fight), you spoke at a ladies' luncheon I was at. You talked about eliminating the word **why** from our vocabulary. That hit home, so I've really tried. "Why" sneaks out every once in a while, but I try to catch myself. Philip has noticed. Last night he told me, "Now that you don't ask me why anymore, I like you a lot more."*

Jessica, Colorado

Conversation Killers

If you want to kill a good conversation—or the possibility of *any* conversation—with your man, here are a few words and phrases that will end it every time.

Why?

If you want to kill a potential conversation in its tracks, just ask your husband, "Why?" It instantly puts him on the defensive.

"But, Dr. Leman," you're saying, "I wish Bob would share his feelings and thoughts with me. It would make me feel more at one with him."

If your guy isn't talking, there may be a reason *why*. Perhaps it's because you're asking, "Why?" If your husband is talking to you and you ask, "Why?" you've effectively torpedoed his attempt to communicate. Asking that is like saying, "Okay, I think you're stupid. You can't figure it out by yourself and you might be wrong, so you better explain your reasoning to me so I can help you."

Knowing that kind of puts a new spin on things, doesn't it? The male ego is much more fragile than you think; it's easily damaged. Because problem solving is so important to your man—it's the way he's wired—it emasculates him for you to ask him, "Why?"

Understand now why he gets defensive when you start in with the why? His shrug or anger means he's blowing you off. He's saying, "Get away from me. I don't trust you if you don't think I'm smart enough to figure it out myself."

What are you saying during this time? "Well"—said dramatically with hand flourishes—"I'm only trying to help. It's like talking to a brick wall."

Now you've got it. Questioning your man will make him like a brick wall. It's a subtle challenge to his male ego that will button up his lips.

Instead, use commands. I know you were told that using commands isn't very relational, but your guy doesn't think of it that way. If you say, "Tell me more about that; that's interesting," your words show interest to your husband. Maybe it's hard to get excited about your husband's 2 iron shot over a tree to the green. But is it too much to say, "Wow, you must have been excited to see that little ball soaring over that tree"? When you say things like that, your choice of words says to your husband, *I care about things that excite you. I care about you.*

It's part of being a helpmate to your marriage partner.

Women Talk

I did it. I shut up. I stopped asking my husband (and my teenage son) mindless questions like, "How was your day?" At first it was hard for me to not fill in the silence around our house. (It made me realize how much I used to talk.) Then it was like magic. Within three days of me shutting up, all of a sudden my shy husband started to open up and share with me about what was going on at work. It led to some intriguing discussions about his feelings of us as a couple and about our financial future. He even shared some things that scared him. Thanks for the tip. We're closer now than we've been in our seven years of marriage (this is my second marriage).

Melinda, Michigan

You Always/You Never

"You are always late. What's your problem?"

"You never do anything I ask you to."

Using the words *always* and *never* can turn any conversation into a one-upmanship contest. When you're in that mode of "you always/you never," it's a sign that there is competition in the marriage. If someone is winning your marriage, you both actually lose because marriage isn't a competition sport. Strip *always* and *never* from your vocabulary right now. You'll be glad you did.

You Should

Women "should" on men a lot, and men don't like to be "should" on. You can improve your marriage by at least 20 percent if you avoid saying "you should" to your husband. Men don't like their choices to be challenged, even in the small things. Here's what I mean.

I've heard two or three women spend 15 minutes discussing a menu. They discuss taste expectations, but they also consider the all-important factors of price, fat content, and their vegetable intake for the day—all of which may launch them into an entirely new conversation on some herb or supplement or even vegetarian cooking.

I don't hear men doing this, do you? Men make a choice and stick with it. We like what we like.

When Sande and I go to Red Lobster, I order the coconut shrimp with piña colada sauce and wild rice on the side. If I go to Caruso's, I get lasagna. I've gone there since 1962 and have never *ever* ordered anything besides lasagna. I know it'll taste good, so why take any chances?

That's not good enough for my Sande, though, who once asked me, "Why don't you try something new?" (Note the word *why*.)

I got defensive, like every guy would. "Well, how would you feel if I tried another wife?"

Her eyes grew wide.

Then I added, "Don't you see that there can be some merit in my always preferring the same thing?"

Ah, now there's the good. Something to chew on when you're annoyed.

When we go to another restaurant, Austin's, I always get a grilled ham and cheese sandwich with tomato soup. Sande "shoulded" me once there too. She said, "You should get this," and pointed to a different item on the menu.

"I don't like that," I said.

"Well, if you ordered it, then I could have a bite," she said in her female logic.

"If you want a bite of it, then why don't you order it?" I said in my male logic.

You see, women like to share food. Men have a far more proprietary attitude. If two men are eating lunch together, it's about as likely for it to snow in July as it is for one man to reach over and grab something off the other's plate. And we never order in committee—"You get this, I'll get that, and we'll split it." It's simply not a guy thing.

Ask Dr. Leman

Q: When I heard you on TV, I understood what you were saying about men and women being different, but what you said still doesn't solve my problem. I *need* words from my husband. I need attention from my husband, and I don't get it. What do I do? I can't stay in a relationship where I'm not getting any attention. How do I get my husband to open up and be the kind of man I want him to be?

Mariah, California

A: You're right. In order for a marriage to survive, you, as a woman, do need words and attention from your husband. But let me ask you, what kind of attention is your husband getting from you? Are you a critical-eyed person? Have you shut down any of his efforts to communicate? The fact you're saying you can't stay in the relationship without some attention tells me this has been going on a long time. By now you're probably starved for attention. But you won't get it by begging or threatening. That will turn him off. He just might be an emotional clod (many men are) who needs some training about what's important to a woman.

Try something this week. Encourage your husband verbally. "Wow, honey, what a great job you did on that. I appreciate it so much." Those words are the takeaway he needs in order to know he's done a good job as provider. Notice that you're not overdoing it, as in, "Oh my goodness, you're just the best person in the whole world." It's like noticing that a child did well on a test at school and coming alongside him to celebrate his achievement. You're not saying, "Oh, you're the greatest kid in the world"; you're focusing on the job done.

Your big, strong guy needs to hear that he's done a good job and performed well in life. But it has to come from you. Not his co-worker. Not his mother. Not his neighbor. You. Start with some kind words and see if they'll lead the way to your husband's heart.

But

It's the instant rebuttal. The immediate cutoff. Your husband is talking, and you say, "But that's not true." Because your coprocessor is wired to respond much more quickly, you could easily outthink your husband and jump in, seeing the flaws in his argument before he's done. But if you do that—jump the gun or jump to conclusions—without hearing the whole scenario, you might miss a very important point he's about to make.

It's very disrespectful to assume what another person is going to say without hearing him out. As soon as you start with "but," you've lost him. Your husband is smart enough to know that whatever comes after the "but" is going to kill everything he just said. It's a wind changer and a relationship killer. "Oh, I'd really like to help you out, but . . ."

So when "but" rises to your lips, think instead of what you could say that would be communication Viagra, an entrée into relational intimacy:

"Tell me more about that."

"Oh, that's interesting."

"I can see why you feel that way. I've felt like that myself."

"That had to be frustrating."

"That seems so unfair."

Little words like these encourage communication. They swing the door open to a heart connection rather than slamming it shut.

Want to *Really* Get Your Man's Attention?

Walk right on up to your man and plant a big one on him. Then stand back a bit, look him in the eye, and say, "I have something to tell you. I love you to pieces, but I really need to tell you something very important." Make sure you touch him as you're talking.

The instant you touched him and kissed him, that man of yours was thinking, *Oh boy. It's my lucky day. I'm going to be rolling in the sack in a few minutes.*

Some of you are saying right now, "Dr. Leman, that's so crass. Why does it have to always be about sex for the guy?" Well, just hold on. We'll discuss that in the next chapter. If you want a new husband by Friday, you have to understand how a man thinks.

Whenever you plant a real kiss on your husband's lips, you have his attention. He's saying to himself, *Oh man, what's next?* And then, subtly, you slip him the commercial announcement. "I just got a call from the Garden Club. I'm supposed to help decorate, but I was also supposed to take Kaycee to her friend's house. I can't do both. I know it's a curveball in your evening, but would you take Kaycee to her friend's for me?" If approached that way, there's no self-respecting man (dysfunctional men aside) who won't do what his wife asked.

Any kind of emotional pat on the back—or pat on the front, for that matter—will keep your husband talking. He will give you a little bit in conversation and see how you respond to it first before

> **Payback**
>
> Do 1 kind thing for your husband; receive 3 acts of kindness from him.
>
> Do 3 kind things for your husband; receive 7 acts of kindness from him.
>
> The ratio return on that investment is pretty high, don't you think?

he tells you more of what he's thinking about. As soon as you get critical with him, he'll shut down. It's best to listen and not talk. Don't query him about anything he says. Wait until he's absolutely done. Then, if you have an issue about anything he said, you can bring it up—again, *after* he's done.

Stroke that man and lead him toward sharing his opinion, and he'll share with you more than you ever dreamed he would. Sometimes a good back scratch or a favorite dessert helps your guy open up too. Have eye contact and listen with that third ear—your heart— and you'll be surprised what you learn. And be careful not to read too much into what he's thinking. Most of us aren't that deep.

What You Really Want in That New Husband

When I spoke at a church in Kansas last month, I told the folks there about the time I sent my daughter roses and a little card to tell her how much I loved her. The female contingency in the audience said, "Ohhhh" in a drawn-out sigh.

"Hey, did you just hear what I did?" I said to the men in the audience. "That little 'Ohhhh' is what your wife is dying to say to you if you do something sweet for her, and chances are good you'll get a lot more than that, because you're touching her heart."

You want that kind of husband, don't you? The kind who will work toward pleasing you? Who is sweet and tender toward you? A man isn't naturally inclined to be that way, especially after he gets the marriage job done. Before, he was on the hunt and was focused on doing all the right things in his singular search to "find the woman." Since he has you now, he must have done a good job on that, right? You should pat yourself on the back. You were well worth the search and the focus that he gave to find you—even if sometimes he doesn't act like it now.

A husband is a little like a lab rat. You know, the rat that runs through mazes where he can turn to the left or the right, and he has to decide which way to run? The rat, after numerous tries, finds out that when he turns right, electric impulses zap his feet. It doesn't take that rat long to figure out that if he turns left, he doesn't get that funny feeling, and he's rewarded by a pellet of food at the end. So of course he's going to go that way. He knows where he's headed, and he's singularly focused on getting the reward.

But what if you changed the rules on that rat? What if you gave him a shock when he turned left, and there was no pellet of reward at the end? The rat would figure, *Well, I guess things have changed around here. Maybe I have to go right to get the reward.* So the little rat will run to the right and find the pellet, and he'll learn to run to the right in the future.

What to Do on Wednesday

1. Give him the Cliffs-Notes, not the whole enchilada.
2. Don't ask, "Why?"
3. Allow him time to process your information. Your coprocessor might be faster, but that doesn't mean it's better in the long run.
4. Remember, he's your lover, not your girlfriend. (And think about it: would you really want that chatty girlfriend around 24-7?)

What would happen, though, if you put that rat through the maze, and no matter what way he turns, you give him a shock? He wouldn't know what to do. Pretty soon the rat would just stay there at the crossroads of the maze, dancing up and down frantically because there's an electric current underneath him, and frustrated because he doesn't know what to do.

That's what happens to most husbands, frankly. They go hide out because they know that no matter where they turn, they'll get an electric shock. So they no longer try.

You, smart woman and brilliant wordsmith that you are, are one of the relational wonders of the world. You could run laps around your husband relationally any day. You need to bring your man along slowly and rather gingerly. He's out of his element, and like that lab rat, he's trying to figure out what to do. You're the one who can give him cues with your words. Your affirming words go much farther than you could dream.

Women Talk

Thanks for your wonderful messages to married couples. What's important to men has just been proven once again in our home. When my husband died last December, I was searching for some important papers and found a strongbox I didn't know about. Inside was every card and note I'd sent him in our ten years of marriage. Most of the time my quiet, shy husband couldn't articulate that he needed me, but now I will never doubt again. What an amazing legacy of love he left me! If people only understood sooner. . . . I wish I had. Thank you for helping people to do so.

M, Minnesota

The other day I met with a male colleague and his wife. We were talking about marriage. The woman looked her husband straight in the eye, reached out her hand to touch him across the table, and said, "You know why we're so happy? Because of you!" It was such a sweet interaction and one I don't see much these days, with so many couples focused on "me."

Now that's one couple I don't expect to see in the divorce courts seven years down the road. I can even envision them sitting together on an old porch swing, wrinkly as raisins, holding hands on their fiftieth anniversary.

Thursday

Think of Him as a Seal Waiting for a Three-Pound Fish

Why making love to your man is a key to who he is and how satisfied he'll be, and what's in it for you.

Have you ever been to the zoo and watched how the seals behave? They're rather comical creatures and seem to crave the limelight. They'll do anything to get your attention. And boy oh boy, the antics they'll perform if they know their handler has a three-pound fish awaiting them . . .

You see, it's all about reward for seals. They live for it. They soak in the praise and the clapping of the crowd and the "well done" fish at the end of the performance.

Seals are a lot like husbands. Did you know that your husband is waiting to perform for you? In fact, he's dying for the opportunity. He doesn't need much encouragement to give you his best shot. Sure, he'd like a three-pound fish every day, but the truth of the matter is, a six-ounce perch would taste pretty good some days.

He'll take anything you give him—to a degree. But when you want to give him your leftovers, you'll find that seal wobbling away as fast as he can go.

Performing for you and your children (if you have any) is what drives your man. He wants to be a good husband; he wants to be a good father. All he needs is the slightest encouragement. Then stand back and watch how resilient and relentless your man can be in providing for you. He may not be able to go from task to task like you do, but there will be a fire in his belly that keeps him going.

When I talk about performing, I'm not talking about the dancing your husband does when he gets out of the shower. (I've been married for over 40 years, so you'd think my wife would enjoy the show, which is why I keep doing it. But I've learned she would much rather listen to a choir singing the "Hallelujah Chorus" than watch me do the renowned towel dance.)

You—and only you—can unleash power in your man. He's waiting to give it to you. He's dying to give it to you. He's all about performing—for you—and he's ready to make it a show to remember.

"Dr. Leman," you're saying, "there you go again. You're talking about sex."

Yes, I'm talking about sex, but I'm also saying that your husband will perform like the stud of all time, working himself to death for you like a salmon doing a 17-mile run upstream if you make him feel respected, needed, and fulfilled. He'll be panting and gasping for air sometimes, but you'll be one fulfilled, satisfied woman who has a happy husband.

So in this chapter, yes, we're going to talk about sex, but we're also going to talk about making love to your man in other ways. What makes your husband feel loved?

As we saw in the last chapter, you're the queen bee of communication. In many ways, your husband is the worker bee. But he wants to take care of his honey. He'll do anything to please you. Anything. Do you believe that? All you have to do is make him feel respected, needed, and fulfilled. He needs to feel special and appreciated. If he does, he'll be that seal that says, "Give me the beach ball, and I'll balance it on my nose for you. I'll perform until you stop clapping!"

The Music That Makes Me Dance

Do you remember the Barbra Streisand song "The Music That Makes Me Dance"? No? Okay, so maybe I'm old, but I love that song. Did you know that *you* are the music that makes your husband dance? No one else. Just you.

For a man, love is centered on the feeling of, *She loves me just as I am—with all my warts and my frailties. There's comfortability there. I don't have to be someone I'm not. She's there for me on the good days and the bad days.*

St. Paul, a very smart guy and one of the great saints of the church, talks about sex in the Bible. I won't quote what he says word for word, so here's the Leman paraphrase: "Your husband's body belongs to you, and your body belongs to him. I want you to do it."[1] If you don't believe me, pick up the Bible and read it for yourself. The great St. Paul goes on to say that in marriage, you should submit to each other.[2] Marriage isn't about one person lording it over the other; it's a matter of submitting *to one another*, trying to please the other. For some of you, that might be quite a different view from what you grew up with.

In general, men don't feel understood. When a woman says to a man, "Don't you understand? I need to feel important in your life. I need you to talk to me," what do you think that man is saying in his head? *Why do you think I go to work every day at 6 a.m. and practically beat my head against the wall? I do it for you and the kids.* Your husband is wired to be a provider and, just like in the caveman days, to bring home the bacon (or the mammoth). He may not be the most thoughtful, communicative person in the world; his way of showing love to you is by providing for your family. That effort seems to consume most men's lives.

You know what the reward for that man is? Sex. In all my years of counseling, I find it extremely interesting that a couple's satisfaction with their marriage is revealed in how healthy their sex life is.

Take a hard-working UPS driver I know. He delivered packages 12 hours a day to provide for his wife and three children.

> *A couple's satisfaction with their marriage is revealed in how healthy their sex life is.*

When he walked down the aisle to say "I do," he was deeply in love with his wife, but something went wrong. When they came to see me in my office, it was clear the wife was not happy with her husband. She felt like all he wanted was sex, and she didn't feel like delivering three times a week. With three kids, she didn't have time to pay him that kind of attention—or any attention, for that matter.

One day the man met someone on his UPS route. The woman he handed the package to was friendly and complimentary. She had an at-home business, so he delivered to her frequently. It wasn't long before he was checking the route sheet and hoping she had a package to be delivered so he could talk with her again. This man was like a dog starving for love and attention.

Within six months, that UPS driver was having an affair with the woman customer. Why? Because she listened to him, touched him, complimented him, and showed him he was worthy of attention.

Now, this guy was solid. He'd even been an Eagle Scout. He never dreamed he'd violate his marriage vows and find himself in the arms of another woman. This is what he said: "It wasn't the sex. It was simply that I found someone who was interested in what I had to say. She listened to me. I felt she understood me. And I felt needed for the first time in 15 years of marriage. I felt appreciated. I was dying inside because I just needed to be needed. And when my wife and I had sex, it always felt like she was doing it because she had to. That she didn't want to."

"Dr. Leman," you're saying, "are you *excusing* this man's behavior? I mean, he had an affair on his wife!"

No, I'm not excusing his behavior. Everyone has choices, and that UPS driver made a devastating one. Now he and his family have to live with the consequences. But I am *explaining* his behavior and why the affair happened in the first place. To stay in a marriage, a man needs to know he is understood, listened to, respected, and needed. He needs to feel appreciated. For a man, marital satisfaction has a lot to do with how sexually satisfied he is.

I've been in the counseling business a long time. I can't recall any couple I've worked with who said, "We have a great sex life," and filed for divorce. I've never seen it, never even heard about it. Being intimate physically with the one you love is an investment that pays great dividends.

You're your husband's one and only. Nothing can take the place of time with you. Your husband is a "hunka hunka burnin' love" (to quote the old Elvis song), and you need to allow him to release that pent-up energy. If not with you, then who?

Women Talk

Sex has never been a big thing in my life. I tolerated it as just another chore I had to accomplish in marriage. I've paid the price for that, and so have my kids. I've separated from my husband on two occasions.

Then a friend of mine put your book **Sheet Music** *in my hands. I didn't buy it. I'd never think of buying a book like that. But my friend said, "I don't know whether you want to read this or not, since you and Sam are separated, but it sure helped us."*

So I read it, and I was stunned. I still struggle with old tapes that run through my head about sex, but I've made a deliberate effort to pursue my husband (who is now living back at home) and surprise him. And now (I can't even believe I'm writing this) I'm actually looking forward to the next time my husband and I share some intimate moments.

Because my dad divorced my mom, I've always felt like a trap door was beneath my feet, and someday, with no warning, it would open up and I'd become a divorce statistic too. Since I decided I needed to make love to Sam (in the bedroom and outside the bedroom), I'm now confident we'll never separate again. Our kids have shown remarkable improvement in their attitudes and behavior, and I have a much happier husband. It took a lot of soul searching and hard work, but now the good days—in which I have little stress in my life—are becoming more and more common. I'm so grateful to my friend who went to the bookstore and bought that book for me. For me, my husband, my whole family—it was a life changer.

Annie, Nebraska

How Much Is Sex Worth to You?

It took ten years of marriage for me, as a man, to find out that sex isn't the most important thing to a woman. Sande and I were talking one night, and I asked her, "What about me turns you on?"

She looked blank. "Well, I don't know."

"What do you mean you don't know? You must know."

She just gave me that Mrs. Uppington stare. "What are you asking questions like that for?"

Then it dawned on me, the psychologist. "Wait a minute. Isn't sex the most important part of marriage?"

"What? Are you kidding me?" she said.

When a Lewis-Harris national poll surveyed women, asking how they ranked various things in their life, sex was fourteenth on the list. Gardening was thirteenth. When I saw that, I thought, *That simply can't be.* But now I know Sande's not off-kilter.

Sex is not the most important thing to most women. But it is to most men, because the act of sex itself with the one he loves validates everything he needs to make him feel prized. To make him say, *Wow. I'm so glad I married that woman. She's all mine.* The smart woman is the one who realizes that sex is a big fish that her seal husband needs to have thrown his way.

I'm not talking about the "Well, I have to do it, I guess, so here I am; pull down my nightie when you're through" kind of sex either. That's degrading to any man. It tells him, "You're not worth the effort. I don't find you appealing at all. In fact,

> *When you tell your husband you want him, that he's the man for you, he instantly feels like Brad Pitt or Matt Damon, even though he may look a little bit more like Danny DeVito or Alfred E. Neuman.*

I'm not even sure why I married you." I'm talking about the "I want you" whispered passionately in your husband's ear. When you tell your husband you want him, that he's the man for you, he instantly feels like Brad Pitt or Matt Damon, even though he may look a little bit more like Danny DeVito or Alfred E. Neuman. He's instantly transformed into the sexiest man on earth, and he'll be willing to give you pleasure like you've never dreamed.

The Great Problem Solver

Women the world over tend to like hugging. They'll hug anything that moves. So when you tell your husband, "Would you just hug me?" why is it that the next thing you know, you're looking up at the ceiling? All you wanted was a hug, a gentle caress, but it turned into something more.

That's because the instant your husband touches you, he has sex on the brain. *Wow, this is the best day of the year. I've gained 15 pounds, but my wife's still coming on to me.*

"What?" you're saying. "All I wanted was a hug. It's been a really stressful day."

But I have news for you. That little Black & Decker engine in your man isn't something you have to crank and crank until it starts. It's instantaneous, it's foolproof, and it will stand to attention almost immediately. It's a fact of biology that men are wired to be physically stimulated, and they turn on quickly. If you walk up behind your husband, kiss the back of his neck, and caress him in the right spots to show you're a ready teddy, then get no response, there's definitely something wrong with your man. He needs a new DieHard. You'd better bring him in to the doctor for servicing.

For a man, sex is the great problem solver. If he had a bad day at work, sex makes it disappear. If your toilet overflowed and ran down into the laundry room and he had to clean everything up, sex fixes the aggravation of that. If the two of you had a fight before dinner, sex once the kids are in bed is the great fix-all. That's because when you have sex with your man, his world is righted again. Sex is the cure-all for a man.

If you are intimate with your husband sexually, he knows he's loved. That act of sex is a release of tension. If you welcome him into your arms, it proves to him that the problem you had—the fight earlier—is solved. Even more, many men get more of a psychological charge from watching their wife experience the joys of sex than from their own paltry little orgasm. By your "oohs" and "ahhs," what you're telling your man is, "I want you. I need you. You're my man. You're a great lover. You satisfy me." That's what makes your man go through life as your champion—even if he does have a little extra inner tube around his tummy. Your man needs to know that he makes a difference in your life.

The problem is that in most marriages, sex becomes predictable. As one woman told me, "He always starts here, goes there, and then ends up there." Wow, gives you something to look forward to, doesn't it? And only on Saturday and Tuesday? Is sex like clockwork in your house? If I was that woman, I'd as soon pull weeds in the rain as have sex. But remember that your man, as we talked about in the last chapter, thinks in linear, logical, lockstep fashion. He simply doesn't think, *Oh, I should get a little creative here and do something different.* No, he thinks, *Hey, I've got this sex thing down. I do this and this and this, and it works. Perfect. Figured it out.*

So if you're bored with your sex life, why don't you be the instigator? Buy a book on married sex such as *Turn Up the Heat* or *Sheet Music*, and slip it into your husband's briefcase or car. Include a note with it:

> Honey, this is just a little something I picked up for you. I think you'll find it great reading. I've read it already too. I'd love to try something you read about in this book. You know me, I love surprises. More than that, I love you, and I'll be waiting for you.

That's a smart woman who's using all the intelligence the Almighty gave her. She's taking the initiative to change things rather than whining about how sick she is of their lovemaking style. Whining and complaining won't get a guy's attention—it'll just turn him off.

But all men love a challenge. Giving him a book with highlighted pages and a note will start his engines revving and his thoughts turning toward you and home. You could try this note:

You always ring my bell, honey, but I'm wondering if you could *really* ring my bell. The kids are going to be at Grandma's tonight, and we'll be alone. You know what I've always wanted? To have sex in the backyard. The kids just put up the tent today, now that it's summertime. How convenient is that? Can't wait to see you tonight.

That will get your man anticipating a wonderful evening with you. He'll swagger through his day thinking, *Hey, I'm desirable. I may be losing my hair, but she still wants me.* He may not be the svelte 23-year-old you married 17 years ago, and he has a belly on him, but you can play him like a piano. And both of you can have great fun doing it. So why settle for predictable when you can have fabulous?

Kiss Your Husband, Peck Your Girlfriend

If you're going to kiss your husband, then kiss him. That little peck on the cheek should be reserved for your girlfriend. It does very little for your husband. If you want to get your husband's engines revving, kiss him with passion. Even if you can't hop in the sack with your husband at that moment, you'll create an environment of sexual excitement and passion that will keep your man coming back for more.

Let's say you're out for dinner with your in-laws, and your father-in-law is telling you for the third time about the great game of golf he had three days earlier. You reach under the table, unbeknownst to your father-in-law, and give your husband's thigh a couple little taps in such a way that, wow, have you got his attention. It's the hint that says, *Hey, let's wrap up this evening.* If you know it's going to be a boring evening, you might even want to say, as you're going out the door to the dinner, "I can't wait to hold you in my arms once dinner's over." That will start his motor running, and he'll tell himself he's the luckiest guy in the world. He'll treat you that way all through dinner. He'll sit there smiling at you and thinking, *Not only does my wife love me and think I'm sexy, but she's willing to go to dinner and hear about golf for an hour from my dad. She can't wait to make love to me. She loves me, wants me, needs me.*

So, what's in it for you? If, in order to make ends meet for your family, your husband needs to paint houses on the weekend besides doing his regular job during the week, he'll do it. If he needs to pick up your daughter from preschool in the afternoon, because you're so exhausted due to your deadlines and need to take a nap, he'll arrange to leave work early and pick her up. Why? Because you've made him the most important priority in your life, so he'll return the favor.

How to Make Love to Your Man

1. Affirm his hard work in providing for your family.
2. Ask for his help and promise him a reward.
3. Be positive even in tough times.
4. Learn to think differently. Marriage isn't about what he's supposed to do or what you're supposed to do; it's a relationship.
5. Get behind his eyes to see how he views the world and what's important to him.
6. Surprise him and take him someplace *he'd* like to go.

The Power of Your Words

I'm convinced the words that you, as a wife, use with your man are so important that they can bring him to a climax of sexual satisfaction. Don't take my word for it, though. Ask your husband, then try it out. "Does it mean a lot to you when I tell you how much I love you, want you, and need you? Or do you get tired of it?"

You know what he'll say? "When you say you need me, I tell myself I'm the luckiest guy in the world."

If your guy is sexually satisfied with you, why would he ever violate his marital vows with some woman from the office or some hooker? Why would he, if he has a lover and a best friend at home who loves him, responds to him, listens to him, and respects him? There's no need to shack up with someone else.

Men will always notice other beautiful women. But the power of your words and your mutual satisfaction in sex is the emotional hook you put into your man that keeps him off-limits and off the market for any other woman.

Your job in marriage is to make your husband feel special. Women thrive on loving words; loving words for men mean sex. A man feels closest to his mate when he's physically intimate. It's the one time he tunes everything else out and reaps the benefit of physical closeness with you. I'm convinced that in the heat of passion, your words alone could bring a man to climax. They're the little rudder that turns the big ship in the direction you want it to go.

I know how busy you are with keeping up a home, perhaps working full-time or part-time, and taking care of the kids. I know sometimes you just don't feel like it. You have cycles to deal with, and stressful relatives. But keeping your man fulfilled doesn't take much. There are times in life when a quickie before dinner does not mean a drink. (See my books *Turn Up the Heat* and *Sheet Music* for lots of wonderful ideas.) Again, you're an intelligent woman. You're seeing the benefits of this. A little bit of your time—even when things are stressful for you—will gain you a husband who wants to please you, who risks sharing with you his thoughts and feelings, and who will do anything to help you. Don't you want that kind of sweet, wonderful man in your home?

Women Talk

After I heard you speak about what a man needs to feel loved, I felt really guilty. I've treated my husband more like a grown son than a husband and a lover. I've always told him what to do and expected him to do it. I never really asked him if he wanted to do any of those things. I didn't tell him I appreciated him for providing for our family. We've had a lot of struggles as a result. It's my fault. No wonder my husband didn't try any longer to help me but just sat watching TV and tuning me out.

The breakthrough in our marriage didn't come until I apologized to him for treating him the way I have for the past nine years. He was so surprised, and a little wary. I think he thought I couldn't change. But I have—at least, I'm trying.

The other night his favorite TV show, CSI, was on, but when I whispered in his ear that I might have other ideas, you know what? He flipped off the TV and followed me with a grin. That's gotta be a first. I'm planning more rendezvous, but don't tell my husband—I want it to be a surprise!

Sandra, Kentucky

Surprise Him

I love the story one wife told me about how she surprised her husband. It was a Friday night, their anniversary, and she invented a reason to take her husband's car for the day. She dropped him off at work and told him she'd pick him up. He had made plans to take her to a nice restaurant for dinner.

After work, he came out of the office building and got in their SUV, then leaned over to give her a kiss hello. Slowly she unbuttoned her trench coat. She had nothing on underneath. "Do you really want to go to dinner right now," she asked, "or would you like to use the hotel room I reserved for us down the street?"

That woman and her husband still think of that time often—12 years later. It's only one of the many memories they've built by being creative in the way they approach their sex life.

Another wife told me that her husband *hated* shopping. It was on the top of his "don't wanna, ain't gonna" list. She needed a new washer and dryer, though, and some other items that she didn't feel comfortable looking for by herself. So her husband had dutifully gone with her to shop. It had taken all afternoon, and he'd about had enough. But she had to go to one more store. She knew her husband would groan if she even suggested going into Target, so she got creative.

"Honey," she said in a conspiratorial tone, "come closer. I want to tell you something."

"What?"

"No, you have to come close. No one else can hear this."

Her hubby leaned in really close. She then touched him, put her mouth right next to his ear so that it almost felt like a kiss, then seductively whispered, "If you go to just one more store with me, I'll do this as soon as we get home." And she mentioned one of his favorite things to do in bed.

Sex can open a man's ears like nothing else.

You think that man had a smile on his face and happily went to the next store? You bet. Ever after, that favorite thing to do in bed became known to them as the Target Special. They've never told anyone what the Target Special is (they didn't tell me either), but whenever this wife wants her husband to do her a special favor, she knows exactly what to say.

Sex can open a man's ears like nothing else.

Romancing the Stone

"Dr. Leman," you might be saying, "I've heard everything you've said in this chapter about men wanting sex, but you're way off track with my husband. He isn't even faintly interested in having sex with me. I don't think his DieHard has worked in years. I have to beg for it, and I'm dying here. Any help for me? Why does it always have to be the *guy* who has to initiate sex? Don't I get some say in the matter here?"

Welcome to the 15 percent club. Fifteen percent of women have a natural inclination to pursue sex. You need sex to feel fulfilled more often than your husband does (or more often than he wants to give it—more on that in a moment). In 85 percent of couples, it is the husband who is the sexual pursuer. But in 15 percent of couples, the woman is the pursuer. If your husband is the great excuse maker when you approach him for sex ("Not now"; "I'm too tired"; "I don't feel well"), consider these reasons.

He Sees Sex as Dirty

Maybe your husband grew up in a very puritanical home, with many rules and the view that sex as an act is bad, nasty, and dirty. If so, it's understandable that those views carried over to his relationship with you. Every time he has sex with you, he hears his dad saying, "Cover yourself up. You're not allowed to walk around this house naked." In these types of homes, there is also little hugging or encouragement. Your husband needs to reorient his view toward sex, but he needs your help.

If he grew up in a Victorian type of home, where sex was never discussed and was put in a bad light, counseling for both of you would help as you work on your sexual satisfaction.

He's Been Abused Sexually

Sexual abuse is unconscionable. When it happens within the bonds of family, the betrayal and hurt and guilt run even deeper. And for a boy, who is never supposed to cry when it hurts and is supposed to "act like a man," sexual abuse is emasculating. It can lead to intense questions about who that man is, and if he's even a man. *What did I do to make that man [or woman] do that to me as a kid?* Sexual abuse survivors often feel ashamed and dirty. The very act of sex triggers horrible memories and images of perverted sex. If this is the case, you and your husband need to seek professional help together.

It will take time and the guidance of a counselor to better understand the issues.

He's a Homosexual Hiding Out in Marriage

This happens more often than you might think. A guy who has homosexual tendencies marries, thinking marriage will cure him. But he has no interest in sex with you, a woman, and images of homosexuality continue to flood his brain. There is no easy way out of this one. If your husband doesn't desire you, you can't make him desire you. No fancy negligees will arouse him.

If your husband admits to having a homosexual relationship or having had one in the past, that's a whole other story. You need to completely remove yourself physically from him. You need to protect yourself. There is no way to create desire where there is none. Your marriage does not have a high chance of success.

He Has a Physical Problem

If you come up on your husband from behind and begin to stroke him in the right spots, but his engines don't begin to rev into full gear within a minute, your husband may need new batteries for his DieHard. There may be a physical problem that you need to get checked out by your physician.

He Feels Threatened by You and Is Learning to Control You

Remember earlier when we talked about controllers? They make you approach them in a very special way. That man of yours has learned to control you by withholding something you want—sex. He's holding it over your head. Usually this control is not just in the sexual arena; it's in all areas of life. Remember, this can be in a very domineering way or in a subtle way. But both ways are still control. So what can you do if you're living in this type of a situation?

1. Stop buying all those fancy negligees. They won't do a thing. Don't torture yourself thinking, *There's something wrong with me because my husband doesn't find me desirable and doesn't want to make love to me. I'll lose weight, I'll get a slinky new gown...* Stop the guilt trip. No matter how much weight you lose, how much you tone up, how "hot" you look, it won't work. Instead, simply stop asking him for sex. Stop approaching him altogether.

2. Talk to your husband about each of the five areas I've just discussed. Tell him that if any of them resonate with him and he wants to talk to someone, you'd be more than happy to be a part of that. Or if he wants to do it alone, that's fine too. Convey that doing something about these areas is extremely important to you and the health and longevity of your marriage.

3. Hit that tennis ball back into his court. Expect that he will follow up. If he doesn't, pursue it more aggressively. Tell your husband, "I need you to pursue what we talked about. Our relationship can't continue the way it is without dire consequences to both of us. It's that serious."

How Do You Show Love?

I always fear the big events in my life. Like my twenty-fifth anniversary, my fiftieth birthday. Those are the markers in life when I expect a more-than-ordinary present from my lovely wife. But here's the kicker: she tends to buy something for me that *she* really wants, and it usually costs a lot of money.

For our anniversary one year, she bought me a jukebox. Now, I love jukeboxes. At the time, I owned four of them. All of them held 45s of music I grew up with—all early rock-and-roll stars. They're the old kind that kids used to kick if the nickel didn't drop through properly. I can regularly hear Little Richard, Chuck Berry, Elvis ("Thank you very much"), and Little Anthony and the Imperials. It's a wonderful reminiscence of my childhood.

But what did Sande buy me? A CD jukebox. I thought, *What am I going to do with this thing?* It was the thought that counted, but I was stumped. (Fast forward a few years, though, and I learned to love it.)

> **The 5 Languages of Love**
>
> Which is your husband's? Which is yours?
> Words of affirmation
> Quality time
> Gifts
> Acts of service
> Physical touch

You know what is the greatest of all gifts Sande ever gave me? A copy of my very first book cover, framed in a lovely wood frame, that said "#1 husband, #1 father, #1 author, I love you." It was a simple gift that probably cost less than $25. But it tickled my fancy. It scratched where I itched. It told me how much she valued me in her life.

The Language of Love

There's an old story about a small church that needed a new chandelier for the entryway of their building. The church constitution said that 100 percent of the congregation had to be in agreement for any major expenditure, and the chandelier was going to cost over $2,000. So they took a vote. It was 99 to 1. They retook the vote. It was still 99 to 1. So they had a congregational meeting. The chairman of the board got up and said, "There is just one holdup. We want to respect the secret ballot in the church, but if that one person is here and would like to meet with me in private about their concerns, I'd be more than happy to do that."

An old farmer in overalls stood up in the back of the church. "I'm the one who voted against it."

"What's your problem with the chandelier?" the chairman asked. "Would you care to share that with us?"

"Well," the farmer said, taking off his hat to scratch his head, "I don't know about any *chandelier*, but what we really need around here is a light in the entryway of the church."

That farmer didn't know what a chandelier was. The farmer and the chairman were talking completely different languages, but both were trying to accomplish the same purpose. Funny story, but true.

It happens in marriage all the time. Men and women speak different languages and have different love languages. If you don't understand what your husband's is, you could be working at cross-purposes, like the farmer and the chairman, and frustrating each other needlessly.

Do you ever get frustrated with not knowing how best to love your man? Many of you probably are familiar with the wonderful work a colleague of mine, Gary Chapman, has done on the five love languages. His book *The Five Love Languages*[3] highlights the fact that each of us receives and gives love differently.

Now, is your husband going to wake up in the morning and just announce to you what his love language is? No, but it's easy to figure out. It's what he complains about, such as "You never . . ." or "You always . . ." or "I don't get to . . ." Men (okay, me too) are known to whine like little puppies when their feet are stepped on.

Chapman says there are five distinct love languages. Let me summarize them for you.

Words of Affirmation

Does your guy excel at paying sincere compliments and offering encouraging words? Does he always have something nice to say about your appearance, talents, achievement, or attitude? If this is your guy's love language, wonderful. You'll get more compliments than the average wife, and they'll be truly meant.

Quality Time

Does your guy show his love by simply being there, spending time with you? Note that there's a difference between simply taking up space next to you on the couch and really engaging when he's sitting next to you. If your husband's love language is quality time, he loves it when you do things together. That's when he feels most fulfilled. Quality-time people are continual daters. I should know, because quality time is my love language. I just love spending time with Sande.

Ask Dr. Leman

Q: I can't stand it anymore. All he ever does is watch TV. I married a couch potato. Any hope for getting him to do anything else?

Angela, Arizona

A: First question: was he like that when you married him? Some guys have a low libido and low energy. Some are downright lazy and don't want to pull their weight. If you married one of those, then . . . well, you married him. What else can I say? You should have seen it coming. But if you've noticed your husband becoming more of a couch potato over the years, something else could be happening.

Second question: is your guy discouraged in his work? A lot of guys hate the jobs they go to every day, but they go because they have to. Little by little they grow more and more discouraged, thinking, *This is not what I signed up for.* So they begin to tune out life, and TV becomes their life. They are fixated on *Popular Mechanics* like it's the only thing in their world.

Third question: does he know his presence matters in your world, or does he feel unimportant or left out? Many men live in Lonelyville. He needs you much more than you'd ever think.

Fourth question: did your guy used to be attentive, open doors for you, write you notes, send you flowers, or do any other affectionate things? If he did, something has happened in your relationship. Life and your marriage isn't working out for him the way he thought it would.

You need to touch your husband, look him in the eyes, and say, "Honey, I'm sensing that you're tuning out life because you're discouraged. Do you feel that way?" That's the best way to start addressing your situation. But you have to do it in a gentle, nonthreatening manner or you'll cause your husband to shut down further.

Gifts

This is my wife's love language. It's easy to spot with Sande. She just loves giving people gifts, and she's very good at it. It gives her great joy to do so. She also loves to receive meaningful gifts, which means I have to give them.

Giving isn't a matter of money. It's a matter of interest—to let you know he's thinking of you during the day. A rose left on your pillow as he lets you sleep in says it all. It's a token of his feelings of love for you. Other gifts can be ones of adventure, such as going on a romantic picnic or skydiving (something you've dreamed of doing for years).

Acts of Service

Many people see love in terms of doing things for others. The rub with this love language comes because often couples don't agree on what each of their responsibilities are—who should do what. Doing what you're supposed to do doesn't gain you any acts-of-service points. You get those points when you do what isn't expected of you, just because you love your spouse. An example of acts of service would be your husband clearing the snow off your car for you each morning so you don't have to, or carrying the heavy laundry basket up the stairs.

Physical Touch

This is my other love language—just ask my wife. I'm a toucher, and I love to be a touchee. By physical touch, I'm not just talking about sex. I'm talking about kisses, hand holding, bear hugs, and back rubs. All the things that make us physical-touch people happy. If your husband's love language is physical touch, he will not feel fulfilled or loved unless he has it—a lot of it.

So what does your husband whine about? That's the key to his love language.

Does he say you never say anything nice about him? Complain that you never write him sweet notes anymore? Then he's a words-of-affirmation man. Sweet words affirm his masculinity. They give him an "Attaboy, you did good. You really pleased me." He needs to hear that you're so lucky to have a man like him as husband, lover, and friend.

Does he complain about the fact that he never has you alone? That you're so involved in your kids' lives that he can't remember the last time you took a weekend together? Then he's shouting at you that he's a quality-time person. Will you take the time to invest in marriage and your mate, or will you continue on the fast track and put him on the back burner? (I can guarantee you that men won't tolerate being put on the back burner for very long.)

Does your husband say, "Well, last year you got me new golf clubs. This year I got a bath towel for my birthday"? Then he's a give-me-gifts type of guy.

Does he say, "You used to make me homemade pancakes for breakfast on Tuesdays, and you never do anymore"? There's your clue. He's an acts-of-service guy.

Does he complain that you never have sex anymore? If so, he's screaming in your ear, "Touch me, make love to me, pursue me." He's a physical-touch kind of guy.

Can you have more than one love language? Definitely. I'm both a quality-time and a physical-touch kind of guy. Sande is a gift-giving and an acts-of-service kind of gal. So why not take another step toward understanding your husband and identify his love language?

What to Do on Thursday

1. Kiss him. Not the peck-on-the-cheek kind, but the I-want-you kind.
2. Play sleuth. Observe your husband. What makes him feel most loved? How can you tell?
3. Say "I love you" in the way that means the most to him.
4. Take a risk. Step out of your comfort zone. Surprise him. (I'll leave that to your imagination.)

I'll Say It Again: Men Are as Dumb as Mud

By the time I asked Sande to marry me, my sister was married and living in another city. My brother was in grad school. No one pulled me aside and said, "This is how you ask a woman to marry you." I had no clue I was supposed to do something romantic—like take her to a five-fork restaurant. So you know what I did? I gave Sande her engagement ring in a field behind my parents' home.

I think back now and shake my head. How dumb I was. Holy crow. I'm glad she said yes.

More than 40 years of marriage later, I've learned a lot about romance. I have the best teacher in the world—my wife, Sande.

You see, a man by nature is a lousy lover. He doesn't understand women; he doesn't know where to start understanding women. He needs you to be the gentle lover who leads him along the way and loves him unconditionally. If you do that, you'll have a husband who comes home and cooks dinner when you have the flu, even if he can make only boxed macaroni and cheese. He'll be the daddy who doesn't mind that the kids adhere to him like honey, and he'll wrestle them while you make dinner. He'll be the one who helps you problem solve the program on the computer, the one who muscles the garbage cans out to the driveway. He'll do dishes in the kitchen with no complaints. He'll rub your back when you ask him, and he'll look at you with love in his eyes.

Now, I ask you, what woman wouldn't want that?

All you need to do is a little clapping, a little encouraging, and your seal will perform to his highest abilities. Just don't forget the three-pound fish at the end for his reward. Take him into your bedroom, lock the door, and give him all you've got.

That's how you get a new husband by Friday—and you'll be a much happier wife too.

Friday

It Takes a Real Woman to Make a Man Feel Like a Real Man

How to open your man's heart, revolutionize your love life, and turn him into the knight you've always dreamed of.

I recently had a conversation with the mom of a fourth-grade girl who wasn't like anyone else in her class. "In my class," the girl told her mom, "there's the Pink Bow girls, who like dolls and dressing up and pretending they're married, and the Hannah Montana girls, who like to pretend they're rock stars. I don't fit in either of those groups. I like to play with the boys so much more. They tell you what they think and don't mess around." That same girl (all 50 pounds of her) was the only girl who would play football with the third- to fifth-grade boys after school.

As the whole group huddled, do you know what those boys who knew her said?

Matt said, "No tackling the girl, got it?"

"Yeah," Corey chimed in. "Only one finger allowed on her."

Those tough boys not only allowed that girl to play, but they enjoyed playing with her. But here's what's interesting: they automatically served as her protectors, her heroes. Did anyone tell them to do that? No, but that was how they were wired. "Protect the girl" is what innately registered in the coprocessors of their brain. They didn't want her to get hurt.

When the girl took the ball and ran with it, all the boys cheered her on. And when they picked teams again, all the boys wanted her on their side. (And this is at an age where boys punch girls to get their attention if they like them.)

Isn't that what you want? A protector? A hero who wants you on his side? Just like those little boys were self-proclaimed protectors of that little girl, your husband (still a boy at heart in a grown-up body) wants to protect you and be your knight—even if you do need to polish his armor from time to time to keep it at its shining best.

Men often run silent, but they run deep, to quote an old movie title. They take in information you give them, mull it over, and analyze it logically from every vantage point they can find. That's also part of their provider and protector instinct. It's just the nature of the beast.

Roll Over, Beethoven, Ms. America Has Arrived!

There are some sensitive areas in this book that you might not like to hear, and this will be one of them. How do I know you might not like what I'm going to say next? Because I'm a veteran of speaking in front of audiences nationwide, and the response is always the same. I've been on *The View* talking about sex. I've been in places where wise men never go. As the old song by Brook Benton says, "Fools rush in where angels fear to tread." Yup, that's me.

Some women bristle at the thought of putting their husband first because they feel that puts them in an inferior position.

Usually there are very good reasons for women to feel this way. (A lot of it has to do with how Daddy treated them; and let's face it, men have wiped their feet on women for centuries, so there's some history here.) But that doesn't mean they have to feel like that. And thinking that way won't help their marriage.

Let me recap what we talked about earlier in the book. Clearly men and women are not the same, but they're of equal social value. When you put your husband first, you're not making yourself a doormat. You're playing the game smart. An NFL coach recently said on camera, "I'm not sure we have the best athletes in the league, but I think we have the smartest athletes in the league." Interestingly, at the time of this writing, that team and that coach are undefeated in the NFL.

> *Some women bristle at the thought of putting their husband first because they feel that puts them in an inferior position.*

In the marriage game, you have to play smart. You have to push aside your socially conditioned responses and indignations. If you continue to think, *Why is it my job to make the first move? Why should I put him first? What is this, caveman logic?* you might as well pull the plug now, since you're going to be a divorce statistic. You have to set aside your girlfriends' incredulity: "You're doing *what* for Bob?"

Think of it this way. Apply the simple (but not easy) principles in this book. Give him a little bit and just watch what he gives you back. He's driven to be the provider. He wants to make you happy, to please you in all things. But you have to make him feel important, special, needed, wanted, affirmed, loved, respected, and fulfilled. Your happy, fulfilled husband will knock himself out to be a good husband to you.

You're a strong woman, a decision maker. You can do eight things at a time with a speed that makes your husband jealous—and a bit intimidated. You even make a wicked PB and J (without the crust) for your firstborn child. So why do you feel threatened, used, or second-class in any way?

Women today wear so many different hats—surgeons, pilots, stay-at-home moms, teachers. They even start publishing companies in their homes. There's no limit to what a woman can do today. And with that seemingly limitless freedom has come one of the biggest dangers to marriage: the "What's in it for me?" question.

I Am Woman, Hear Me Roar!

If you want to have a new husband by Friday, you need to understand the tremendous effect you have on your husband. The words you say, the way you touch him, the respect you give him, the way you listen to him—all those things influence your husband greatly.

> *If you don't think you need a man in your life, then don't marry one.*

If you don't think you need a man in your life, then don't marry one. Just live the single lifestyle. There are lots of folks out there who love being single—coming and going whenever they wish, with only their fish to feed. No one's fighting over the remote control, their checking account has their name on it, and all they have to think about is themselves.

There are a lot of married people today who are living singles' lifestyles. But that's not a partnership. It's a roommate situation.

It used to be that men were the clear-cut leaders in the family. But today it's the women who are making the decisions—about how money is spent, how the bills are paid, etc. I ask you, does it really matter who's in charge of the finances, as long as the electric bill is getting paid and you make sure you have heat in the middle of the winter?

Research shows today that the woman is the bill payer instead of the man, who was the bill payer just 20 years ago. This brings up all sorts of questions about leadership in marriage.

When I talk about leaders, I love to use the analogy of sheep.[1] A shepherd has a unique call and way of tending and guiding his sheep. We think sheep are dumb, defenseless animals, but they're smarter than we think. If someone dressed a different person in the same clothes as the shepherd wore, then digitized the first shepherd's call so it sounded exactly like him, those sheep wouldn't be fooled. They may look at the new shepherd, but they wouldn't come to him. Those sheep would follow only the shepherd.

Let me ask you. Would you have any problem following a good shepherd who was there for you through thick and thin? Who wasn't squeamish about going to Walgreens to buy "light days, windy days, heavy days, elastic with sticky tabs and without zippers, rebar-enforced, smooth-cornered" whatever-they-are when you need them? For a man to do that, he has to care more about you than about any embarrassment to himself. Is this the type of man who would treat you as a doormat? No.

So why such a big deal about leadership? One of my buddies always jokes, "My wife appointed me leader years ago." Is marriage a competition to you? Do you have to "win" the last hand? I'll tell it to you straight. If someone is "winning" your marriage, then you're both losing.

Do you want to live happily ever after or not? "But I don't look good in one of those princess gowns with the puffy sleeves," you say. That's not the point. The point is, do you want to be loved, respected, cared for, provided for, and protected by your husband? Do you want him to respond to your needs? That's what the principles in this book, if followed, will gain you. That's what's in it for you. The other way will head you down the road to anger, bitterness, disillusionment, and divorce.

Women Talk

I've been a fan of yours for years. I thoroughly enjoyed **Born to Win***, because that book is my life story. I'm so good at detailed work, I love numbers, and I love to figure things out. I also know I have that critical eye.*

We had a crisis at school last year. Our twin girls, who are very bright, were doing extremely poorly in school. Finally we figured out that they weren't finishing assignments because they feared the criticism of good ol' Mom. That hit hard.

My husband has paid for that big-time as well. I've seen it in his eyes, and he gets cold and quiet.

I'm working hard to keep my critical eye in check. Before I react in a situation, I begin to think about how I would have reacted, and make a new plan to respond instead. When I'm frustrated, tired, and stressed, I have to admit I slip back into the critical eye, but I've done a 180-degree turnaround. I'm now the first to say, "I'm sorry" to our twins or my husband. Thanks for the great insight. It's leading to great results.

Naomi, New Mexico

Take a Peek

Take a peek over your shoulder. Do it right now. Is your mom or dad there, peering over your shoulder? Could those footsteps behind you be your dad or your mom checking on you? Just how did you learn to be the woman you are today?

Your private logic—the way you look at the world—was formed while you were growing up. How did your dad treat your mom? How did your mom treat your dad? Did your mom use her verbal acumen as a billy club over her husband's head to get him to do things around the house? Did your dad verbally or physically abuse your mom? Or did you grow up in a picture-perfect home where

178

Dad and Mom never fought and modeled mutual submission, mutual respect, and love?

Few of us grew up in those picture-perfect homes. Most of us are carrying around some baggage as a result. You brought to your marriage a certain number of expectations about who a man is. If you grew up in a lousy environment and didn't have a good relationship with your dad, your husband will pay for it. Why? Because you'll tend to view him through the same lenses you viewed your dad through. In fact, how you view your father will color your perspective on everything I suggest in this book.

When I suggest that you give a little time and make your husband a priority, what's your gut response? Is it "Why should I?" or, "Hey, I know I need to do something different. That's a good idea. I can see why it's important."

If you're in the "Why should I?" camp, chances are good that you didn't have the kind of dad you needed, and that has formed your negative view of men in general. Your poor husband doesn't have a chance. No matter what he does, you'll shoot him down.

Is your husband paying for what another man did (or failed to do) in your life? Are you dissing your husband because your father dissed you? What have your experiences with men, particularly your father, been in the past?

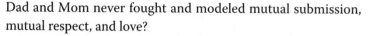

Did Daddy do you wrong?

Could you possibly be part of the problem? Did Daddy do you wrong? If so, now's the time to let go of the grudge, before it ruins your marriage. Go to your husband. Tell him, "I'm sorry. I just realized that I've treated you as if you've done me wrong all these years, just because of what my father did to me. I've been so wrong. I don't want to do that anymore, but I need your help. I can't do it on my own. I love you very much, and I know you're not my father. I'm sorry I treated you like you were. Can we start over?"

It all starts with submission—submission to each other.

The Fighting "S" Word

I'll say it up front: men, be submissive to your wives.

Do I have your attention? I'm old, I'm a bit on the portly side, I have five children and two grandchildren, and I'm now the proud carrier of a Medicare card—but I'm not as old as you think I am.

As soon as I use the word *submission* with an audience, you know what happens? The women start to growl, the men start to slap high fives. Now why is that?

Women hate the word *submission*—and with just cause. I get up before a group of women at a banquet and announce my topic—"How to Be a Submissive Wife"—just to get a rise out of them, and I do. If looks could kill, I'd be riddled with an assault rifle in two seconds flat.

> *Women hate the word **submission**— and with just cause.*

I love the word *submission*. I've learned, as a man, that there are many who would say, "Hey, Leman, you're the leader, the head of the family." But I know that if I'm going to be the man my family deserves, I need to be submissive to my wife. If I'm her leader, I have to be submissive to her. I have to know her—and all the idiosyncrasies about her.

Why can't mutual submission be something to strive for rather than something to be feared? For those of you who are people of faith, the submission mission is about being submissive to God in all things in your life, which in turn allows you to be submissive to each other. Nowhere in the Bible does it say that women should be subservient or submissive to men. Good ol' St. Paul is clear on that: *both* should be submissive to each other, for that is what marriage is all about.

But whether you're a person of faith or not, I'll state it bluntly: men should love their wives so much that they are willing to take a bullet for them. They must be willing to die so that their wives can keep breathing. (And yes, I know men who would do that for their kids as well.) That's what a real man does. Real men from the New York City fire department ran into those burning buildings on 9/11. Real men with families of their own went in as heroes because they knew how much they were needed.

But real men are not easy to find today.

As a psychologist, I am acutely aware of the fact that many couples entering into marriage today came from dysfunctional families. They're unable to submit to anything; they rebel against even the idea. If you have a husband who didn't grow up in a family where Mom and Dad listened to each other, respected each other, and loved each other, and where put-downs flew on a daily basis, what makes you think it will be different in your marriage? Truth is, the little boy he once was, he still is. Show me the kid he was, and I'll show you the husband he'll be.

A few situations might change that—health issues, traumatic experiences, spiritual experiences—but in most relationships, what you see is what you get. Some men will take advantage of a submissive-natured woman and treat her like a second-class citizen. She's the one most likely to develop the martyr personality, and friends look at her and say, "I don't know how you do it." She gets psychologically fed through putting up with all the garbage from her husband. But should she? Absolutely not.

A lot of people think the Bible teaches that women are to be submissive to men. That is not the case. What St. Paul says is that we are to be submissive to one another.[2]

What does mutual submission look like? It means including your husband in decisions. If you've decided you're going to re-decorate the house and surprise him, and that he won't say anything because he doesn't care and the house is really your domain, stop right there. Chances are, he does care. He may not know (or care to know) all about color coordination, but he certainly does care about the overall look of his home.

This week, Sande asked me if she could write a check to a young woman who is preparing to go to Africa on a missions trip over Christmas. "Are you kidding me?" you may say. "Your wife has to get permission from you to write a check?" No, Sande doesn't have to ask me anything. Her name is on the checkbook, just like mine. But out of respect for me, the bill payer in the home, she asks me. She tells me specifically what she'd like to do: "I'd like to encourage that young woman by sending her a donation for her trip—I'm thinking a couple hundred dollars. Is that okay with you?" I always thank her for asking.

You see, it's all about mutual submission and respect, for the good of both of you. Since I'm the one paying the bills, I deserve to know what money she's spending so I don't get bushwhacked by an overdraft on our checking account.

Do you respond to your husband out of respect? Or do you order him around and treat him like a child? Some women treat their husbands as a third or fourth child, then complain when they act like one. Go figure.

A smart woman is one who addresses her husband with respect as they sit at the breakfast table, sipping coffee on a Saturday morning. "I know it's not the time, and I know you're so busy at work that we couldn't do it right now, but someday I'd like to get that backyard finished. I realize we can't afford it at this point, but someday I'd love to get it done."

If her husband is healthy psychologically and not damaged by an abusive background, he'll take on that challenge. Such words are just the type of kerosene a man needs to light his fire. He'll turn into that 4-year-old who wants to surprise his mommy and make her happy.

What did that woman do right? She gave all the qualifications. She was straightforward in her request. You can bet that man will go out of his way to please her. And isn't that what mutual submission is all about?

Many women like foot rubs and head rubs. Not my lovely wife, Mrs. Uppington. She doesn't like to be rubbed. She likes to be scratched—lightly, with just the tips of the fingernails—in the shape of a big S. How do I know that? Because I'm submissive to my wife. When I walked down that flower-strewn aisle, my lifelong job became to understand Sandra. To love her as *she* wants and needs to be loved.

In the same way, when you said "I do," your job became to please, respect, and honor your husband. Not an easy job, but it's simple. And the rewards are simply incredible.

Ask Dr. Leman

Q: My husband is always late. Last week I told him our daughter's play was at 4:00. He got there at 4:45, when it was over. He didn't even get to see Megan's solo—her first ever at a school play—and she started crying. How can I explain to my daughter about her daddy missing something so important to her?

Deanna, Toronto

A: You don't have to explain anything. Your husband does. Put the tennis ball on the side of the net where it belongs. Were you late? No, your husband was. Your daughter may ask you, "How come Daddy didn't get to my play on time? Danny [her younger brother] was there, you were there, but Daddy wasn't." The smart mom would respond, "Honey, I don't know. You're going to have to ask your daddy that." Let your husband see your daughter's tears and hear her questions for himself. That's the only way you'll find him showing up on time for events.

Adjust Your Dream

What was your original dream about what a good husband is? When you look back on it now, did you have a bit of a Pollyanna attitude? He was going to be the romantic knight who would sweep you off your feet and into his house, deliver fresh flowers every day with a flourish, and regale you with affectionate language on an ongoing basis. If that was your dream, you need to adjust it, because it's simply not gonna happen. You're asking your male creature to be something he's not.

Recently our church had two separate events—a men's night and a ladies' night. For the men's night, a basketball coach came to speak. We had one-and-a-half-inch pork chops that were out of this world. When it was time to eat, a guy said (in typical male style), "Okay, guys, listen up. We're going to go through this door, pick up food, and come back through that door."

While I was waiting in line with all the other chumps, I noticed a couple of bowls of salsa on a table. The chips were just laid out on the table—not on a tablecloth, not in bags, just dumped out on the table by the salsa. I thought, *Oh, Mrs. Uppington wouldn't like this*, and started chuckling.

Last Sunday night was the ladies' night at the church. The brochure that came three weeks in advance announced that it would be "a time for you to get away from the busyness of the holiday season and have time for yourself, away from the stresses and cares of life."

After the church service on Sunday, I—along with the other men in the church—was handed a note:

Hey, it's a surprise. We're going to serve the women dinner at their ladies' night tonight. Wear a white shirt and tie and meet in the Promiseland (kids) section at 5:00.

I thought, *Hey, I can do that—show up and serve dinner.* But I didn't own a white shirt. So I wore a blue shirt with a red tie and looked as nice as I could.

That night I arrived promptly at 5:00 as ordered, and we guys walked over together to where the ladies were having their dinner.

When I saw how the place was decorated, I couldn't help but smirk a little. Guess who had decorated? Mrs. Uppington herself. I had to admit, the whole atmosphere was wonderful.

When I strolled in, tray in hand, I heard applause from table 9. My wife and three of our daughters were there, grinning ear to ear at seeing me dressed up and serving dinner in my blue shirt and red tie (mind you, all the other guys did wear white shirts). I mumbled to myself all evening, "Serve from the left, pick up from the right." Thankfully I didn't stumble, fall, or make a fool out of myself.

At the end of the evening, the women sold the lovely centerpieces that my wife had worked on forever. Contrast that with the chips dumped out on the table at the men's night.

> *I don't want to change genders. I enjoy watching football and belching after eating pizza. I'm the man I want to be.*

You can spend a lifetime trying to make your man into something he's not. Or you can let him be the man he is. I don't want to change genders. I enjoy watching football and belching after eating pizza. I'm the man I want to be.

Your husband wants to be your champion. He wants to know he's appreciated for bringing home the bacon—or the Northern pike. So you don't like fishing. Your idea of a fish is a salmon, lightly grilled, in a fine restaurant with at least three forks. But you know your guy loves fishing. Could you find a fishing lodge your husband would love to go to that has a nice fireplace, where the two of you could snuggle up together? Sure, he could take his buddies, but with all due respect to them, you're the one he'd rather have along.

If you gave me a choice of hanging out with the guys or going someplace with my wife, I'd take my honey any day.

Having a new husband by Friday isn't rocket science. What you put into something is what you tend to get out of it. You and

What You've Said about Your Guy

What You've Said about Your Guy

The little things I love: "My husband never looks so sexy to me as when he crawls out, his hair sticking up all over the place, from the tent in the living room that he set up to have a daddy-son night with our 5-year-old twins."

"My husband makes fresh-squeezed OJ every Saturday morning and brings it to me in bed, just because he knows I love it. It makes me feel so loved. Move over, Leonardo DiCaprio, you don't have anything on my man."

"I love it when my husband plays board games with the kids and gives me a breather on Friday nights."

your husband bought that flat-screen TV, which doesn't do a lot for your marriage, does it? So why not spend some time and money to invest in each other?

He's Not Your Girlfriend—but He Is Your One and Only

I'll say it straightforwardly again. He's your husband, not your girlfriend. Can you let him be male? That was the gender you agreed to marry, right?

You're not going to find your husband wiping tears as he tells you about a situation at work. He's not going to open himself up completely. He's going to tell you a little at a time and test your response. For instance, it took me eight days to tell Sande about a urological problem I was having because I knew she'd worry. As her protector, I didn't want that to happen. So I didn't tell her until the doctor visit was over and we already had a solution.

Remember that you have a lot of girlfriends, but he doesn't have anyone. Just you. And sometimes your kids get in the way of your intimacy (just as they do for couples across the planet). You're too pooped to whoop or have anything remotely resembling an intimate moment.

So what do you do? You can ignore your guy's needs. You can exploit his needs and manipulate him to do something for you later that night. (Both will end up with the same disastrous result

186

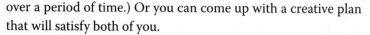

over a period of time.) Or you can come up with a creative plan that will satisfy both of you.

Your husband isn't your girlfriend, so he doesn't want the blow-by-blow about your day. But he does need to know that he's your man. That he's a priority in your life. So if you're talking to your husband and your children interrupt you, say sternly, "You need to wait. I'm talking to your father." They'll get the message. Those little whippersnappers aren't dumb. *Oh, I get it. Dad's the number one guy around here.* Even if you were interrupted that time, you've set the record straight on who comes first. Your husband will see that, and he'll know that not only do you say he's your champion, you act on it. He needs to know that you're in his corner.

> **What to Do on Friday**
> 1. Think back to your own childhood. How did your dad treat your mom? How did your mom treat your dad? How did your dad treat you? How have those early experiences influenced the way you interact with your husband?
> 2. Choose to act differently. Believe that you will see results.
> 3. Tell your husband you're glad you married him. That he's your man.
> 4. Treat him as your hero, and he'll act like it.

What's in It for You?

I did a survey a few months back in one of my "Mother Stress" programs. I asked the group of women what the top three stressors in their life were, and they all agreed, in this order:

Kids

Time (the lack thereof)

Husband

Notice that in the top three you didn't see work, household chores, or finances? Now isn't that interesting—especially when those are things that we all have to do?

Think about it for a moment. If you win the cooperation of your husband, who better to help with those three stressors?

Kids—Who can help juggle all you have to do with them?

Time—Who can help get done what you can't get done, even if you're the multitasking wonder of the universe?

Husband—Ah, now that's the subject of this book. If you do just a little, you'll get a new husband by Friday, and he'll help you get everything else done. He'll be your hero who will knock down brick walls for you with his bare hands.

There's the kind of stress that happens when you slam on the brakes in traffic and almost hit a car. Adrenaline rushes through your body, and your heart feels like it's in your throat. But miraculously, within 20 minutes your body goes back to normal. Everyone has stress like that, and there's nothing you can do about it.

But there's another kind of stress that's prolonged and just doesn't go away. It's the stress of being Velcro Woman—the woman everything and everyone sticks to. No matter how hard you try to shake it, it never goes away. It's the kids, the lack of time, and the annoying husband that can put you over the edge. It's like going to the mall to shop all day and leaving the lights on in your car, and

For Men	For Women
How to Juggle	*How to Juggle*
Use 1 hand.	Use both hands.
Throw 1 ball straight up in the air and catch it as it comes down.	Throw 5 balls up simultaneously in the air and neatly catch all 5 until you have a perfect sequence going.
And you wonder why you're intimidating to men.	

when you come out nine hours later, the car won't start; the battery is exhausted. Ever read news accounts about actresses collapsing on stage? They end up being hospitalized for exhaustion.

That doesn't have to be you. Win the cooperation of your husband, your helpmate, and you get instant relief from the three top stressors in your life. He'll take time off work to see his daughter perform her first piano solo. He'll volunteer to drive the bus with 14 preschoolers to a local supermarket for a field trip. He may not do it like you would, but he'll get the job done. And the preschoolers don't know the difference between store-bought and homemade chocolate chip cookies for their snack anyway.

> **Something to Think About**
>
> Tell your husband, today and every day, one thing you appreciate about him. Touch him as you say it, and the message will get through loud and clear.

Keep in mind that there are women out there who would give anything to have a real man. So do everything you can to keep your man, to encourage him, and to make him feel respected, needed, and fulfilled.

Having a new husband by Friday is all about perception. When I was a little boy, I distinctly remember telling my mother that when she made a sandwich for me, it tasted better than when I made it for myself. There's no way that sandwich could have tasted better—it was a PB and J on white bread—but in my mind it did, because she made it just for me. She also made tomato soup and put a little butter on top. It would spread out and add a great flavor. Tomato soup with butter is still one of my favorites today.

You see, our perception of things makes a difference. A 31-year-old woman I know admirably juggles three small children. She also routinely runs everything by her husband.

"What?" you might be saying. "Can't this woman make any decisions on her own? Is she one of those women who always sign checks 'Mrs. William J. Jones' instead of 'Sally Jones'? Like she doesn't have any identity separate from her husband?"

Frankly, I wondered the same thing. But as I watched that young couple interact, I was pleasantly surprised. The way both husband and wife submitted to each other was beautiful to watch. When the wife ran things by her husband, she was doing so out of respect—not because she had to. She didn't want him to be surprised or to hear about something thirdhand that affected her or their life as a family. The husband, on his part, was constantly doing all kinds of things to please and serve his wife—and got great joy out of doing so.

Your knight will polish up his armor for you if you give him the least bit of encouragement. He longs to be your hero. The little boy in him wants you to be happy with him, proud of him.

So he's not perfect. You're not perfect. Life's not perfect. But why not enjoy the gift you have in that husband of yours?

Women Talk

As a senior VP of a bank, I supervise 36 employees, attend regional meetings all over the Southeastern US, and have done very well in my career. I made great money and had everything the world said was important, but inside I was dying because I was a lonely person who lacked direction. I avoided any confrontation in my marriage because I knew I wasn't successful in that arena. So I poured all my energy into my work.

There were many nights when my husband simply fended for himself. Why he stayed with me for over 12 years is beyond me, but he did. And now I've finally made the big decision—I'm 37 years old—that I want to have a family. I've already begun to put things in motion to quit working and stay home ... if I get pregnant.

You spoke in May at the regional in-service for our bank. I became haunted with the truth that one of the ways I protected myself from getting hurt by any man was to keep my husband at arm's length and to hide behind my success, busyness, and prowess in the banking business. But my success in business did nothing for my soul. And here I had this sweet soul mate who didn't have a soul to share with.

I told my husband the truth and apologized for hurting him. Step by step, I've begun to honor him—at last!—in our marriage. I finally understand why people say that marriage is great. I could never say that before. I had to humble myself before my husband and begin to think "us" instead of "me." I did the few basic things you suggested, and I no longer fear my marriage will come to an end. I not only have a new husband, I'm a new wife.

Jana, New York

Give Yourself a Shot

I flew in to speak in Elmira, New York, got to the hotel, and unpacked my bags. Before I left for my meeting, I dug around for the little bottle of Scope in my briefcase. Guess what else I found? A note from my wife, who was flying in a bit later to meet me and drive to Michigan. Now, remember that we've been married forever, okay? Here's what the note said:

> Hi, sweetie. I know you're going to do a great job. I can't wait to see you on Wednesday. We're going to have so much FUN [she'd put a squiggly line under "FUN"].

I know what that means in Baptist-ese. Sande, because of her conservative nature, will never write anything too explicitly. But she took the time to put a note in my briefcase.

If you want an insurance policy for a husband who travels, tuck in a funny card or a love note. Caring goes a long way. Maybe Hallmark got it right after all: "When you care enough to send the very best."

Caring takes work. But anything that's worth it takes some work.

Caring ought to be fun work. I can testify to that, having been married for over 40 years—all in a row to the same woman. Sande and I have always put a priority on each other as husband and wife first, then on our children as our second priority in terms of people on this earth.

What do you want to invest in? In your dying breath, I hope you won't be asking the question, "Why am I dying?" If you do, you're in trouble. You should be asking, "Why did I live the life I did?" If you've lived the life you wanted to, and you know the port of call where you're going, you'll have no worries.

Maybe Hallmark got it right after all: "When you care enough to send the very best."

Why not live that way every day? Right now, as I write a few notes for the end of this book, my wife is at the Great Indoors. "Honey, I'll just be about 20 minutes," she says.

I smile. I've been married long enough to know better. "I'll stay outside," I say. "You just take your time."

You know why I say that? Because it's her day, not mine. And I chose to spend it with her. Sande puts me first and respects, needs, and fulfills me, so I put her first.

Is putting your husband first always easy? No. But it's simple. Having a new husband by Friday starts with changing you—your attitudes, your actions. Do you really want to please your husband?

You may have to work harder to make your union a healthy one, because of your background. You may have to come to a clearer understanding about your past—how it affected you then, how it affects you now, and how you interpret your husband in light of it. Some marriages, frankly, aren't fixable—especially if there is brutality, mental illness, chemical addiction, etc., involved. But that's also a decision you'll need to make with the tools I've given you.

We all have the same 24 hours of the day. Where does your time and energy go, and to whom? How different is your life now from when you were dating? (Understanding that will help you understand why your husband acts like a 4-year-old sometimes in trying to seek your attention.) It's presumptive arrogance to believe that your man is going to be satisfied while you put your kids first, then your sister, then your job, then your friends—then him. And that man

> *We all have the same 24 hours of the day. Where does your time and energy go, and to whom?*

is supposed to be patient, understanding, kind, loving, and helpful in the midst of being dissed? Men can take women for granted, but women can also take men for granted. Is this true of you?

In your daily grind of activities, remember that your husband isn't the enemy. He's your helpmate. If you've slipped into the mommy track, it's easy to forget you have a longer, far more lasting track that's called the marriage track. Once your little caboose leaves home, you and your husband still have to look at each other. So why not establish a foundation now that will last a lifetime? Talk to him, ask what he thinks, get his opinion, let him help you solve problems. Develop your "couple power" (two are better than one). If you do the few simple things well in this book, you'll have that hero you've longed for—the knight who would ride into battle to rescue you. "Need some help? I'll be right there," your knight will say.

> *"Need some help? I'll be right there," your knight will say.*

Why not ask your husband today, "Would you make a list of the things I could do to be a better lover, spouse, and friend to you?"

Having a new husband by Friday is simple, but it's not easy. It all starts with you. Get to know your man—how to approach him, talk to him, stroke him. Know when to back off, know when to speak up. Feed him, entertain him, listen to him, laugh with him, have great sex with him. Be a nurturing friend and understanding of his maleness. Pray with him. Share your joys. Share your sorrows. Come alongside him.

In other words, treat your husband as you would like him to treat you. If you do, you'll have a soul mate for a lifetime.

One night I leaned down to kiss Sande good night and could barely bend over. It was unusual that my raccoon-hours wife was in bed before me, but that day she was stressed out. She was so tired she could hardly move.

She laughed. "Honey, the good thing in all of this is that we're going to grow old together."

Yes, we will, and I'm going to treasure every minute with the woman of my dreams. There's nothing better than growing old with the one you started the journey with.

So enjoy this creature called a man who does his nails at a red light, whose idea of fine food is a steakburger with fries, who thinks he could play in the NFL if he could get himself in shape. Enjoy him because he's *your man*.

One morning, as I waited in a Dodge dealership in Westfield, New York, I asked three of the guys who work there what one thing each of their wives could do to make them feel like they really are her knight in shining armor. I couldn't believe what they said.

"Prepare my favorite dinner for me."

"Pray for me."

"Keep doing what she does."

"Nope," I told the third guy, "not specific enough."

He scratched his grizzled cheek. "She looks out for me. She keeps an eye on my diet. I'm a diabetic, so that's really important."

Those certainly aren't the responses you'd expect out of "real men" who like to get their fingernails dirty working on cars, are they? Frankly, I thought one of them would say, "Allow me to bring my deer head into the house," "Dance for me in that slinky red number," or "Drop her pants right there at the front door." But that's not what I heard.

Interestingly, these men are in their fifties, and they've all been married for over 20 years. They're solid, mature men who have a strong faith in God. They're in marriage for the long haul.

President John Kennedy once said, "Ask not what your country can do for you; ask what you can do for your country." Now apply that to marriage. "Ask not what your husband can do for you; ask what you can do for your husband."

How would your marriage change if you applied that principle? I guarantee you it would get you a new husband by Friday.

The rest is up to you.

What Would You Do If . . . ?

Take this quick quiz to find out if your gut is on the money or off the mark. (See page 205 for the answers.)

1. You really need an answer to something by tomorrow. The situation simply can't wait longer than that, and you need and want your husband's input. What do you do?
   A. Call him at work and tell him about the situation, then ask him what he thinks.
   B. Drive to his office or job site and tell him you must have an answer.
   C. Ask a girlfriend or his boss's wife what she thinks he'd say.
   D. Wait until after he's come home from work, had his dinner, gone potty, looked through the mail, and vegged out a little in front of the TV, and then tell him about the situation and ask for his input.

2. Your husband won a trip to Hawaii at work because he met his sales quota this quarter, and you're invited to come along.

You've been married 25 years. Neither of you has been to Hawaii before. What do you do?

A. Go along and just enjoy being with your husband and seeing what he does.

B. Ask your sister or a friend to join you on the trip so you can shop instead of being bored while your husband is in all those business meetings.

C. Take this as a unique opportunity to take along two of your three grown children, who live in California and whom you see only four or five times a year.

D. Refuse to go on the trip and stay home because you have responsibilities to tend to and can't leave them.

3. You woke up late, hit the showers fast, got the kids out the door to school, and are dressed and ready to whiz out the door when you notice . . . *Uh-oh.* Your husband is looking at you like he's Bullwinkle the Moose's first cousin, and he's one interested fella. But you have ten things to do before 9:00 and an appointment across town at 10:00, then you're heading to your part-time job. Sure, your husband may have the day off after working seven days straight, but you don't. You can't believe the look he's giving you. The look that says, *Hey, baby, let's have some fun.* And you know he wants the whole enchilada. What do you do?

A. Glare at him and say, "Do I look like I want to fool around? Can't you see I'm dressed already and I need to get out the door?"

B. Cajole him by saying, "Honey, not now. But if you're patient, I have some time in early March available."

C. Walk up to him, grab his antlers in a very affirming manner, and then use your creativity. Then lean over and whisper in his ear, "And there will be more where that came from—a whole lot more—when I get home tonight." End your little session with a passionate kiss before you walk out the door.

   D. Just ignore him and whiz out the door. After all, you've been married 12 years. He can wait.

4. You find a note your husband wrote at 6:00 in the morning to your daughter, who's going away that day for a retreat. It's the sweetest, kindest, most touching note a dad could write to a daughter. What do you do?

   A. Show your girlfriends the note over lunch.

   B. Wait until you see your husband that night, give him a warm hug and a passionate kiss, and look him in the eye. Say, "That was an awesome note you wrote our daughter. I know she really appreciated that. I can't believe how lucky I am to be married to a man like you!"

   C. Frame it and hang it in your daughter's room so when she comes home it will be on her wall.

   D. Call your husband at work and tell him how sweet the note is, and that it made you cry.

5. Planning family vacations is important to you, and you have something very special in mind for this summer. You want to get it scheduled. You asked your husband two days ago but haven't gotten anything even remotely resembling an answer out of him. What do you say?

   A. "Hey, bucko, I asked you a question two days ago, and I expect an answer."

   B. "I feel very hurt and disrespected that you haven't shared with me any of your thoughts about our trip."

   C. "Hey, honey, could we revisit that question I asked you the other day? About our possible vacation? Could you give me a little idea of what you're thinking? I'd really appreciate it."

  D. "Now listen, buddy. I don't know if you realize it, but that trip is seven and a half months away, and I need to make plans. I have to get going to get the best plane reservations."

6. You want to show your husband you really care about him. What do you do?
  A. Give him a 20-minute dissertation during the middle of Monday Night Football about how important he is to you.
  B. Make him his favorite meal with his favorite dessert.
  C. Send the kids to Grandma's for the night as a surprise and plan a hot rendezvous.
  D. Show that you respect him, need him, and enjoy fulfilling him as your lifelong partner.

If you don't get 5 out of 6 right on this quiz, go back and read the book again.

Epilogue

It's Not Easy, but It's Simple

Have a new husband by Friday? Is it possible?

To tell you the truth, it's a scam. You can have a new husband by *Wednesday* if you do it right.

Making changes in your marriage isn't easy, but it's simple. It all starts with you, and your motivation and desire to make things work in your marriage. That's because you are the very best teacher your man could ever have. You're closer to life—you see in 3-D color while he sees in tunnel-vision black and white. You're able to juggle multifaceted projects, personalities, and endless to-do lists while he's singularly focused on one task at a time.

There's no doubt that your man is much less complex than you are. After all, he doesn't have to deal with the "monthlies" you do or any of those hormone changes. But never mistake your simple male creature for being simpleminded. Far from it. Your man is continuing mulling things over in that computer between his ears—things you may never dream he'd be thinking about or planning.

But when it comes to his needs, he only requires a few basic things from you to keep him purring like a contented kitten:

Show him respect.

Show him he's needed in your world.

Listen to him, and honor his opinion.

Affirm his masculinity.

Don't ask him, "Why?"

Choose your words carefully—and streamline them.

Pursue his body at will—and put the sizzle and fun back into your relationship.

Having a great marriage is all about mutual respect and getting behind your spouse's eyes to see how he or she views the world. It's about serving each other—a 100/100 relationship, instead of a 50/50, "what can the other person do for me?" partnership.

I've given the topic of having a new husband by Friday my best shot. The rest is up to you. Sure, following these principles will take a little time and some forethought. They may mean stepping out of your comfort zone and taking a risk. But isn't your husband and your marriage worth your best shot? Aren't *you* worth it? Don't you want, in your heart of hearts, a stud who would knock down walls for you?

It all starts with these simple principles. If you follow them, you'll get the miracle turnaround you're longing for.

I guarantee it.

The Top Ten Countdown to Having a New Husband by Friday

10. Respect what he says.
9. Tell him how important he is in your life.
8. Tell him how much you need him in your life.
7. Pursue him.
6. Don't correct him or make fun of him, *especially* in front of others. (Your tough guy is much more sensitive than you think he is.) Don't be a bone digger (unearthing past misdeeds and throwing them in his face).
5. Don't talk down to him. He's your husband, not your child (even if he does act like it sometimes).
4. Touch him physically. One caress can last a long time and will *really* get his attention.
3. Say nice things about him and to him. (Good gossip about your guy is like an emotional hug.)
2. Eliminate the words *why*, *never*, and *always* from your vocabulary. (When you speak in extremes, you stop honest communication cold.)
1. Think about what you're going to say and divide it by ten.

What Would You Do If . . . ?

Quiz Answers

1. You really need an answer to something by tomorrow. The situation simply can't wait longer than that, and you need and want your husband's input. What do you do?
   A. Call him at work and tell him about the situation, then ask him what he thinks.
   B. Drive to his office or job site and tell him you must have an answer.
   C. Ask a girlfriend or his boss's wife what she thinks he'd say.
   D. Wait until after he's come home from work, had his dinner, gone potty, looked through the mail, and vegged out a little in front of the TV, and then tell him about the situation and ask for his input.

Answers: If you chose A, not a good idea. Your husband isn't a Johnny-on-the-spot thinker, nor is he good at multitasking. When he's at work, he's at work, and when he's home, he should be at home. Putting him on the spot will only frustrate and irritate him.

If you chose B, you're going to start World War III. No guy likes being interrupted in his work with a demand for a "now" answer. You're also likely to embarrass him in front of his co-workers.

If you chose C, look out. No self-respecting guy wants you to ask someone else what he would think. He wants the skinny from you—and straight from you—without you going to anyone else for their opinions first.

If you chose D, what a smart woman you are. You might even ramp up the interest in the conversation by making him his favorite dessert and touching him to get his attention.

2. Your husband won a trip to Hawaii at work because he met his sales quota this quarter, and you're invited to come along. You've been married 25 years. Neither of you has been to Hawaii before. What do you do?

   A. Go along and just enjoy being with your husband and seeing what he does.
   B. Ask your sister or a friend to join you on the trip so you can shop instead of being bored while your husband is in all those business meetings.
   C. Use this as a unique opportunity to take along two of your three grown children, who live in California and whom you see only four or five times a year.
   D. Refuse to go on the trip and stay home because you have responsibilities to tend to and can't leave them.

Answers: If you chose B, guess what you're really saying to your husband? "You have to be the most boring man I know, and what you do is boring too. I have to have someone to keep me entertained while you do your thing. Who wants to be stuck in a stuffy old business meeting when there's beautiful Hawaii to discover? Beaches to enjoy? Shopping to do?"

If you chose C, you're thinking relationally, as a woman is wired to do. You're thinking, *Wow, what a great opportunity. The kids would just love this, and we'd have a free room. This is our only chance to get to do something like this as a family.* But think about it from your man's perspective. He has shared you with those children all these years. Now is his chance to receive a pat on the back for work well done, with the woman he loves right by his side. What could get better than that?

He's also thinking, *Boy, I can't wait. Just the two of us alone in beautiful Hawaii, with a room all to ourselves. The things we could do together in that room. . . . Hey, I bet she'd look beautiful in a red nightie. I better check into that . . . and I'll call ahead to have her favorite flowers in the room and some Godiva dark chocolates on the pillow too. This is going to be INCREDIBLE.* See what I mean? Behind the scenes, your big boy is working hard to please you, so don't dash his hopes. Isn't your marriage worth spending time with just him?

If you chose D, you might as well march yourself into a divorce court now, because that's where you're going to end up. No guy can take being second fiddle (or third or fourth) for long. So you have responsibilities. Everyone does. But would the world cave in if you took a respite from them for a few days to enjoy your husband? It would mean the world to him, and it would do a world of good in your relationship to get away together.

If you chose A, you certainly have your priorities straight. Chances are pretty high that, in another 25 years, you and your husband will be sitting on the porch swing, holding hands and still looking googly-eyed at each other. Now that's love. Putting each other's interests first and spending time together as a top priority is the glue that holds marriage together—and makes for a lot of fun along the way.

3. You woke up late, hit the showers fast, got the kids out the door to school, and are dressed and ready to whiz out the

door when you notice . . . *Uh-oh.* Your husband is looking at you like he's Bullwinkle the Moose's first cousin, and he's one interested fella. But you have ten things to do before 9:00 and an appointment across town at 10:00, then you're heading to your part-time job. Sure, your husband may have the day off after working seven days straight, but you don't. You can't believe the look he's giving you. The look that says, *Hey, baby, let's have some fun.* And you know he wants the whole enchilada. What do you do?

A. Glare at him and say, "Do I look like I want to fool around? Can't you see I'm dressed already and I need to get out the door?"

B. Cajole him by saying, "Honey, not now. But if you're patient, I have some time in early March available."

C. Walk up to him, grab his antlers in a very affirming manner, and then use your creativity. Then lean over and whisper in his ear, "And there will be more where that came from—a whole lot more—when I get home tonight." End your little session with a passionate kiss before you walk out the door.

D. Just ignore him and whiz out the door. After all, you've been married 12 years. He can wait.

Answers: If you chose A, you just told your husband that he's the last priority on your to-do list, and you just shut down any romantic notions he's going to have toward you for a while. Is that really worth it? Couldn't some of those errands wait? If you skipped one or two and had a roll in the sack with your husband, I bet both he and you would go about your day a lot happier.

If you chose B, it's because you, as a woman, are the schedule queen of the universe. You're the multitasking genius who somehow makes all of life work not only for yourself but for everyone in the family. Maybe you're saying "not now" because you know there's no time to take another shower. So why not use your creativity? What you could accomplish in five minutes or less probably wouldn't cramp your schedule too much. And your husband would be grinning ear to ear like a cross-eyed Siamese cat as he even does some of your errands for the day.

If you chose D, simply said, your marriage is in trouble. If you ignore your man, he'll find someone else who'll listen to him, respect him, and fulfill his needs. Is that really what you want?

If you chose C, you know what your man needs—and you'll still step out the door looking like you could be on the cover of *Glamour* magazine. Even better, you've left behind an emotionally satisfied man who is glad you can be the flexible woman you are. And guess what? When you get home that night, he might even have the house cleaned and dinner made—and he'll be all too willing to help you pack the kids off to bed just a little early. That ought to put a smile on both of your faces.

4. You find a note your husband wrote at 6:00 in the morning to your daughter, who's going away that day for a retreat. It's the sweetest, kindest, most touching note a dad could write to a daughter. What do you do?
   A. Show your girlfriends the note over lunch.
   B. Wait until you see your husband that night, give him a warm hug and a passionate kiss, and look him in the eye. Say, "That was an awesome note you wrote our daughter. I know she really appreciated that. I can't believe how lucky I am to be married to a man like you!"
   C. Frame it and hang it in your daughter's room so when she comes home it will be on her wall.
   D. Call your husband at work and tell him how sweet the note is, and that it made you cry.

Answers: If you chose A, you just might embarrass your guy. Sure, it's good to pass on good gossip about what your husband does (that will make him puff up happily when he hears about it), but that note revealed a sensitive side of your husband that he's comfortable showing only to you and your daughter. Some things are best not shared, even with good girlfriends.

If you chose C, you're majorly overdoing it. That note is a special correspondence between dad and daughter. Let your daughter decide what she wants to do with it. It doesn't need to be emblazoned on the wall for the world to see.

If you chose D, you're interrupting your man's workday with an emotional tidbit—something he, as a guy, is not comfortable dealing with at home, much less at work, where he has to be on task and focused.

If you chose B, you hit the nail on the head. You're meeting your husband's top needs of being respected, needed, and fulfilled just in that little interlude. And I bet he'll think, *And I'm pretty lucky to be married to a woman like you too.*

5. Planning family vacations is important to you, and you have something very special in mind for this summer. You want to get it scheduled. You asked your husband two days ago but haven't gotten anything even remotely resembling an answer out of him. What do you say?
    A. "Hey, bucko, I asked you a question two days ago, and I expect an answer."
    B. "I feel very hurt and disrespected that you haven't shared with me any of your thoughts about our trip."
    C. "Hey, honey, could we revisit that question I asked you the other day? About our possible vacation? Could you give me a little idea of what you're thinking? I'd really appreciate it."
    D. "Now listen, buddy. I don't know if you realize it, but that trip is seven and a half months away, and I need to make plans. I have to get going to get the best plane reservations."

Answers: If you chose A, then "buckette," you're in trouble. Would you want him to approach you that way? The golden rule applies: treat others as you yourself would want to be treated.

If you chose B, you play a good martyr, don't you? In playing the role of the hurt and offended one, all you'll succeed in doing is shutting down your husband. You're not going to get anything out of your guy. No way, Jose.

If you chose D, then you're not your husband's partner, you're his worst enemy. You're treating him like he's the one stopping all your best-laid plans. Then again, are you sure they're your best-laid plans? Have you thought them all the way through, as your husband is probably doing?

If you chose C, you're right on the money. When your husband receives information from you, it goes in the computer between his ears. He then needs to process that information, and that will take time. That's the nature of the male beast you married. If you approach him with respect, in this way, you'll find out he truly has been mulling it over—and I bet he has some good ideas.

6. You want to show your husband you really care about him. What do you do?
   A. Give him a 20-minute dissertation during the middle of Monday Night Football about how important he is to you.
   B. Make him his favorite meal with his favorite dessert.
   C. Send the kids to Grandma's for the night as a surprise and plan a hot rendezvous.
   D. Show that you respect him, need him, and enjoy fulfilling him as your lifelong partner.

Answers: If you chose A, I have two things to say to you: you need to learn the importance of timing, and you need to shorten your word count. Monday Night Football is sacred to most guys, so don't mess with it. You'll just irritate him by talking during the play-by-plays (even if you're saying wonderful things) or obscuring his view of the big screen. You might get a word in edgewise during commercials or halftime, but then those times are usually his potty and snack breaks. So why not pick a time when you can have his full attention, without football competing? Then touch him gently and you'll get his attention. Limit your words to about a tenth of what you'd usually say, and I guarantee you he'll hear every one.

If you chose B, you're right. The old adage is true: the way to a man's heart is through his stomach. There's nothing better to a guy than coming home and smelling dinner cooking and cookies baking, and having a wife who's welcoming. No, you don't have to be Susie Homemaker. Some women love to cook; others hate it. I know a woman who can't bake a lick, but she can whip up a mean batch of chocolate chip cookies from those little tubes from the grocery store. But putting yourself out a little for your guy will reap big dividends for you and your relationship. You'll have a man who's willing to do anything for you.

If you chose C, you're right. There's nothing like a little one-on-one time with the man you've chosen for a lifetime. Everything else—dusting, reports for work, and walking the dog—can wait. Put on that little number that's been waiting in the back of your closet and see how much fun you and your spouse can pack into an evening.

If you chose D, you're right. You truly understand the top three needs of your man—to be respected, to be needed, and to be fulfilled. That's the recipe for a lifetime of marital bliss.

If you don't get 5 out of 6 right on this quiz, go back and read the book again.

Notes

Monday: Secrets Revealed

1. Paul Candon, "Brain Structure May Influence Male-Female Behavior Differences," New York Times Syndicate, December 15, 1999, http://nytsyn.com.

2. Jane Everhart, "Male, Female Differences Can Impact Treatment Regimens," New York Times Syndicate, December 28, 1999, http://nytsyn.com.

3. Ibid.

4. Jennifer Cox, ed., "Understanding the Human Brain," *Children's Britannica*, Encyclopedia Britannica, Inc., 1996, 136–41, December 7, 2008, http://www.sfu.ca/~dkimura/articles/britan.htm.

5. "Left Brain Memory Activity Stronger in Women, Right Brain in Men," OBGYN.net, August 7, 2004, http://www.obgyn.net/newsheadlines/womens_health-Neurology-20040807-77.asp.

6. "Right Brain v. Left Brain," *Herald Sun*, October 9, 2007, http://www.news.com.au/heraldsun/story/0,,22556281-5006123,00.html.

7. Ibid. For a fun test of whether you're right-brain or left-brain dominant, go to http://www.news.com.au/dailytelegraph/story/0,,22744841-5012895,00.html.

8. Dr. Lena Sun, "Gender Differences in Pain Sensitivity and Responses to Analgesia," *Journal of Gender-Specific Medicine* 1 (September 1998): 28–30.

9. Everhart, "Male, Female Differences."

10. Dr. Sandra R. Leiblum, "Sexual Problems and Dysfunction: Epidemiology, Classification, and Risk Factors," *Journal of Gender-Specific Medicine* 2 (September–October 1999): 41–45.

11. Ibid.

12. Ibid.

13. Jean Kerr, quoted in Robert Andrews, *The Columbia Dictionary of Quotations* (New York: Columbia University Press, 1998).

14. The Barna Group, "Christians Are More Likely to Experience Divorce Than Are Non-Christians," December 21, 1999, www.barna.org.

15. Sharon Jayson, "Women Rule the Roost, and That's OK with Men," *USA Today*, September 25, 2008.

16. Sharon Jayson, "Gender Equality Settles in at Home, but Not in Certain Jobs," *USA Today*, September 25, 2008.

17. Michael Gurian, quoted in Lynn M. Johnson, "Parenting: Babies and Toddlers," www.about.com.

Tuesday: Creatures from Another Planet . . . or Creatures of Habit?

1. Karen Sherman, "Right-Brain Women, Left-Brain Men," ThirdAge, December 21, 2006, http://www.thirdage.com/today/love-romance/right-brain-women-left-brain-men.

2. For more on pleasers and controllers, see my book *Pleasers: Why Women Don't Have to Make Everyone Happy to Be Happy* (Grand Rapids: Revell, 2006).

Thursday: Think of Him as a Seal Waiting for a Three-Pound Fish

1. See 1 Corinthians 7:3–5.

2. See Ephesians 5:21.

3. Gary Chapman, *The Five Love Languages* (Chicago: Northfield Publishing, 1995).

Friday: It Takes a Real Woman to Make a Man Feel Like a Real Man

1. For more information, see my book with William Pentak, *The Way of the Shepherd* (Grand Rapids: Zondervan, 2004).

2. See Ephesians 5:21.

About Dr. Kevin Leman

An internationally known psychologist, radio and television personality, and speaker, Dr. Kevin Leman has taught and entertained audiences worldwide with his wit and commonsense psychology.

The *New York Times* bestselling and award-winning author of *Have a New Kid by Friday* and *The Birth Order Book* has made hundreds of house calls for radio and television programs, including *Fox & Friends*, *The View*, Fox's *The Morning Show*, *Today*, *Oprah*, CBS's *The Early Show*, Janet Parshall's *America*, *Live with Regis Philbin*, CNN's *American Morning*, *Life Today* with James Robison, and *Focus on the Family*. Dr. Leman has served as a contributing family psychologist to *Good Morning America*.

Dr. Leman is also the founder and president of Couples of Promise, an organization designed and committed to helping couples remain happily married. He is a founding faculty member of iQuestions.com.

Dr. Leman's professional affiliations include the American Psychological Association, the American Federation of Television and Radio Artists, the National Register of Health Services

Providers in Psychology, and the North American Society of Adlerian Psychology.

In 1993, he was the recipient of the Distinguished Alumnus Award of North Park University in Chicago. In 2003, he received from the University of Arizona the highest award that a university can extend to its own: the Alumni Achievement Award.

Dr. Leman attended North Park University. He received his bachelor's degree in psychology from the University of Arizona, where he later earned his master's and doctorate degrees. Originally from Williamsville, New York, he and his wife, Sande, live in Tucson, Arizona. They have five children and two grandchildren.

For information regarding speaking availability, business consultations, seminars, or our annual Couples of Promise cruise, please contact:

Dr. Kevin Leman
P.O. Box 35370
Tucson, Arizona 85740
Phone: (520) 797-3830
Fax: (520) 797-3809
www.lemanbooksandvideos.com
www.drleman.com

Resources by Dr. Kevin Leman

Books for Adults

Have a New Kid by Friday

The Birth Order Book

Turn Up the Heat

Sheet Music

Making Children Mind without Losing Yours

Have a New Husband by Friday

Born to Win

Sex Begins in the Kitchen

7 Things He'll Never Tell You . . . But You Need to Know

What Your Childhood Memories Say about You

Running the Rapids

What a Difference a Daddy Makes

The Way of the Shepherd (written with William Pentak)

Home Court Advantage

Becoming the Parent God Wants You to Be

Becoming a Couple of Promise

A Chicken's Guide to Talking Turkey with Your Kids about Sex
(written with Kathy Flores Bell)

First-Time Mom

Keeping Your Family Strong in a World Gone Wrong

Step-parenting 101

The Perfect Match

Be Your Own Shrink

Say Good-bye to Stress

Single Parenting That Works

*When Your Best Isn't Good Enough**

Pleasers

Books for Children, with Kevin Leman II

My Firstborn, There's No One Like You

My Middle Child, There's No One Like You

My Youngest, There's No One Like You

My Only Child, There's No One Like You

My Adopted Child, There's No One Like You

My Grandchild, There's No One Like You

DVD/Video Series

Have a New Kid by Friday

Making Children Mind without Losing Yours (Christian— parenting edition)

Making Children Mind without Losing Yours (Mainstream— public-school teacher edition)

Value-Packed Parenting

Making the Most of Marriage

* This book is being reissued by the publisher as *Why Your Best Is Good Enough* in March 2010.

Running the Rapids

Single Parenting That Works

Bringing Peace and Harmony to the Blended Family

Available at 1-800-770-3830 or www.lemanbooksandvideos
.com or www.drleman.com

Every kid in **America** will **hate** this book...

Revell
a division of Baker Publishing Group
www.RevellBooks.com

New York Times Bestseller
Over 300,000 in print

Have a
New Kid
by Friday

How to Change
Your Child's
✓ Attitude
✓ Behavior &
✓ Character in 5 Days

Dr. Kevin Leman

Bestselling author of *Making Children Mind without Losing Yours*

...*but* **moms** *will love it!*

Family expert Dr. Kevin Leman reveals in this *New York Times* bestseller why your kids do what they do and what you can do about it—in just five days!

Have a New Kid by Friday so you can enjoy your weekend!

Change your life
with these great resources

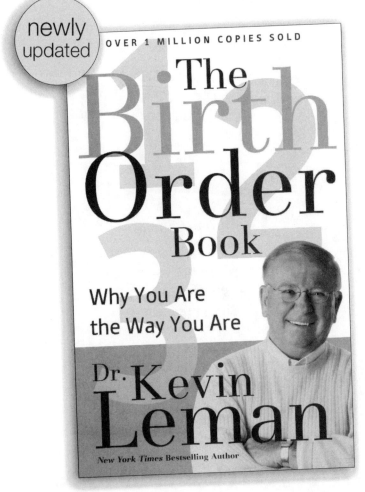
Firstborn? Only child? Middle child? Baby of the family?
Find out what your birth order means to you, your relationships, and your career in this updated edition of the
bestselling book from Dr. Kevin Leman.

ℛ Revell
a division of Baker Publishing Group
www.RevellBooks.com

from Dr. Kevin Leman

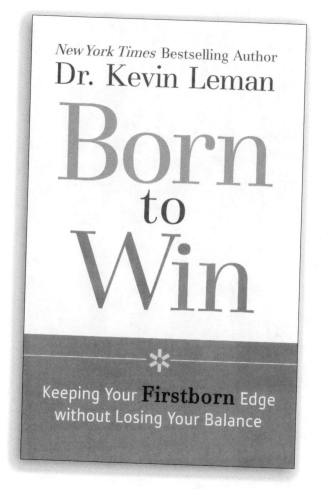

Dr. Kevin Leman helps firstborns understand their natural advantages for the highest level of personal success.

Make your marriage *sizzle*

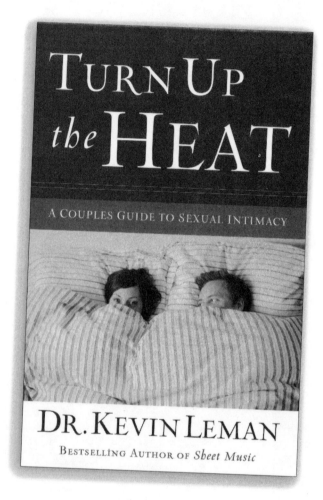

With his trademark humor and advice, Dr. Leman offers frank answers to the questions all of us have about sex.